TRUE STORIES

COWBOY BOB MCCLARY

True Stories © 2025 by Bob McClary

All rights reserved. No part of this book may be reproduced in any form whatsoever, by photography or xerography or by any other means, by broadcast or transmission, by translation into any kind of language, nor by recording electronically or otherwise, without permission in writing from the author, except by a reviewer, who may quote brief passages in articles or reviews.

ISBN: 979-8-9892410-2-6

Ebook ISBN: 979-8-9892410-3-3

Cover photographs by Christie McClary.

The author's publication was assisted by Full Bloom Publications, an independent services provider: www.fullbloompublications.com.

To the McClary family.

SOME STORIES

Kind Words for This Book   vii

1. Mothers are not good to practice roping on   1
2. Musicians sometimes argue   2
3. Learning about alcohol   3
4. Steer ridin'   6
5. The show must go on ... Daddy as a woman   8
6. Horse-breaking lessons   11
7. Having neighbor trouble   14
8. Wild cattle catchin'   16
9. Stampede downtown   19
10. Horses don't shop good   22
11. I don't like ants   25
12. Let's walk   27
13. Sittin' and thankin'   31
14. Shoeing horses is a dangerous job   33
15. Whoa!   37
16. Uncle Sam   39
17. Monkey running barrels   44
18. Cowboys in a hurry, not good   48
19. Snakes   50
20. Horse stuff   61
21. Pets don't need to be around horseshoeing   67
22. Goat sense   69
23. Burnin' brush   71
24. Trying to fix ol' spoilt horses is interestin'   75
25. Cats   80

26. Teeth	88
27. Electricity and horses ... not good	93
28. Sale barn horses	96
29. Dancin' girls	101
30. Havin' fun can get serious	105
31. Mad women	108
32. Machine guns	113
33. Bad shot	116
34. Cows and soldiers	119
35. Cowboy on the beach	122
36. A cowboy and his city pardner	126
37. Ride the right horse	129
38. Sometimes a clown ain't funny	132
39. Be nice to your little sister	135
40. Cowboy fishin'	138
41. Cowboy babysitter	142
42. The doctor	144
43. Acting	147
44. Rodeo rappin'	157
45. Guts and overcoming	162
Parting Words	167
Thank Yous	169

KIND WORDS FOR THIS BOOK

Storytelling has a long history, dating back to ancient mankind. Before the development of written language through visual pictures, recording notes of cultural life was done through stories. Many of these stories were told to infants to form cultural justice and roles in a society. For example, the stories of the three pigs, Goldilocks, and Cinderella all communicate forms of social status and power in primitive forms. Other cultures I have studied have similar underlying principles, such as the early Basque Europeans and Native American tribes of Navajo and Cherokee cultures. Storytelling has been noted as a therapeutic approach, whether in annual conferences of storytellers, articles written in alternative medicine journals, and the respect given professors such as Dr. Angeles Arrien for her studies.

Bob McClary belongs in the highest order of storytellers, especially because his stories describe authentic experiences. Like most underlying principles taught in these stories, there are conclusions to be drawn: of *what not to do* and *what to do* in crisis situations. As a measure of concentration, there is usually humor in the lessons.

Storytelling in cowboy culture has been popularized by Hollywood sagas and saturated by political and racial violence. This has subtracted from the important struggles of developing skills and relationship roles as part of that culture. For me, it has been an honor to see and understand the important roles within the cowboy vocation and family relationships. Although I have lived in Texas and participated in specific rituals of cowboy life, Bob's stories brought me a more accurate understanding of this culture as a viable source of American history.

I invite you to appreciate Bob's voice as you read the stories with a sense of adventure, creativity, and love. Bob has an instinct for the storytelling art. It takes an artist to apply phrases and accents of a cultural language, to deliver stories with full appreciation of the experience, and to make reading them such a delight. I invite you, the reader, to experience the messages herein and enjoy the humor of them.

—Dr. G. Frank Lawlis
   Psychologist and author of *Healing Rhythms*

1

MOTHERS ARE NOT GOOD TO PRACTICE ROPING ON

I GUESS I need to start out with the dearest, sweetest mother anybody could ever have in their whole life. When I was little, by the time I could walk, I was roping. Roping everything that walked: cats, dogs, chickens, didn't make no difference to me—I would rope it. One day, my dear, sweet mother came home from work. Of course, she had worked hard her whole life. Now, I guess something happened that day. She was in a bad humor when she got home and I was hiding around the corner when she walked in. When she came by me, I heeled her—roped one foot. That was definitely the wrong thing to do. She almost fell down, and she taught me a lot about roping at that particular moment, when she took that rope off. Because she took that rope and pursued me to whip me with it, telling me that one thing you do not do with a rope is do not ever, EVER rope your mother ever again.

2

MUSICIANS SOMETIMES ARGUE

ALSO, I always liked music, but I think my mother, well basically, she ended my musical career. I probably could have been a huge star if this had not happened. I got a mouse guitar, and my older sister got a mouse guitar, for Christmas. Naturally, the guitars were just exactly alike. But we were playing them one afternoon and I decided that hers sounded better than mine. So I got hers, and she got mad. We were fighting over them two mouse guitars, when once again my dear, sweet, lovable mother came in the house. I guess the same thing happened to her that teed her off at work, because once again, she was in a foul humor. I was the culprit of the guitar fight. She took that guitar away from me, whooped me over the head with it and tore my guitar all to pieces. So, I've been kind of scared and a little bit leery of a guitar ever since then. I think that's exactly what ended my musical career.

3

LEARNING ABOUT ALCOHOL

OF COURSE, my dear, sweet daddy, he taught me a whole lot of life lessons. Liked to have killed me several times, but other than that, I lived through them. Me and him, we sure had lots and lots and lots of fun our whole lives together. One time we were in Marlow, Oklahoma. He was going to be roping calves at a big calf-roping up there.

A friend of ours that was putting the roping on called him up and said, "I need you to come up here a day early and help me pen these cows and calves." He had hurt his back and he could not ride. Me and daddy load up, I'm about five, maybe six years old, and I take my horse along with me. We get up there and spend the night. That man explains to my daddy about going out and gathering those cows and calves.

The next day, there was about six other cowboys that showed up. And we go and gather the cows and the calves, and we pen them. Late that evening, we sorted them cows off from them calves. This was before all these nice living-quarters trailers, because we had bed rolls, we built a fire, and all of us cowboys sat around that fire and had something to eat: some beanie weenies, some other stuff, or some bologna sandwiches.

We were just having a great big ol' time. I was sitting on a big concrete log and there's another ol' boy there with a fiddle. He thought he could fiddle, and he was a-fiddling. When we finally got tired of his fiddling, I told him to stop. There was another fine gentleman who went to his truck, came back, and had with him a little fruit jar that had some water in the fruit jar. And I should have known something was kind of funny about that water, cuz when he unscrewed the cap off that fruit jar, the cap just came all apart. It just fell all apart in his hands.

They went to passing it around and everybody took him a nice little drink of water. I sat right beside my daddy, and he took him a nice drink of water. I heard two of them guys say, "That sure is smooth. That's really smooth." I've never understood what this *smooth* meant. But my daddy took a drink of this nice water and he handed it over to me –I was kind of thirsty anyway—so I took me a big gulp of that water. But it wasn't water, it was White Lightning.

And let me tell you what, my eyeballs rolled back in my head. I fell off the back of that log and my daddy caught that fruit jar, and I didn't have no air left in the state of Oklahoma anywhere. I thought I was going to lay right there and die, for sure. And all them cowboys was a-laughing. That kind of brought me back around. I learned a whole lot about White Lightning that particular night. And the main thing I learned is that I dad-blamed sure did not want no more of it.

4

STEER RIDIN'

I FINALLY GOT a little older and all along about seven years old. I thought I wanted to ride steers. That just looked like so much fun. And I aggravated my daddy for a week about riding a steer. He said, "No, Bob, them steers will hurt you. You don't wanna ride bulls later on. You don't want to start riding steers. You'll get bucked off, them steers will step on you, and they'll hurt you. Just please don't ride no steers—just rope."

We had a big ol' calf there, weighed about four-hundred pounds. And I just kept on with my daddy all week long, "I sure want to ride that steer." Finally, he got all that he wanted of that, so he went out there and roped that steer, snubbed him up to a post, got me a rope, set me up on that thing, and turned him loose. And sure enough, he bucked me off. I guess I rode him about probably twelve foot before he bucked me off and stepped on my belly.

Steer ridin'

My daddy went and got the steer again, led him back up there, got him back to that post, tied him up, and throwed me up there again. This time I rode him about eight foot, then he bucked me off, run over the top of me, kicked me in the side, hurt my hip, hurt my ribs, and I really kind of had all I wanted. But I really thought for sure that I could guaranteed ride that rascal if I had a saddle on him. My daddy gathers the steer back up again, goes in the barn, gets my saddle, throws that saddle on that steer, and I try him again. I did ride him a little bit further, maybe twenty feet. He bucks me off again, kicks me in the side of the head—as if he liked to knock me out.

Well, I'm hot and sweaty and I've got dirt all over me. I'm bruised up and I commenced to tell myself that I believe my daddy's right. I don't think I need to ride no steers. And I told Daddy. He asked, "You want to ride him again?" I said, "No, Sir. I think you've convinced me that I don't need to ride no steers."

He said, "That's good, because you ain't got the talent to ride steers. Take this here rope and that's what you need to do from now on, is just rope." And sure enough, I forgot all about riding steers.

5

THE SHOW MUST GO ON ... DADDY AS A WOMAN

I GOT A LITTLE BIT OLDER, and we had an arena that was a good arena, but we didn't have any chutes in there yet. There was a rich man in Dallas who knew my daddy because my grandpa used to call square dances back in the Depression days. This rich man, he put together a square dance team on horseback, and my grandpa would go and call them square dances. They would perform all over the country, in rodeos, at every show in the world. My daddy got to go all the time because my grandpa couldn't see very good at night to drive. They were getting ready to go to the rodeo at Stamford, Texas, over July the Fourth to perform out there.

The day before they left, this lady fell off her horse and had a bad wreck, she hurt her knee and it was all swelled up. She couldn't go to Stamford, and they said, "We got to have a replacement for that lady." But they didn't have nobody else who knew the routines except my daddy from

The show must go on ... Daddy as a woman

watching all the time. They told him, they said, "You're going to have to go out there and you're going to have to be the woman."

They get out there and he wasn't too thrilled about that, but my grandpa made him do it. They got to Stamford, got all set up to stay out there four days. Everybody camped out back then. It was a huge rodeo—still is to this day. They take my daddy up there to town, to the beauty shop. And fixed him up with a wig, got some makeup on him, and put some other things that kind of stuck out there where women stick out every now and then. They dressed him up like a woman. They come back to the rodeo that night, all get on their horses, and they go out there and they perform. My granddad called that square dance, and it was a huge success. And everybody, the whole crowd, just loved it. For four days they did that. And nobody know that a particular woman happened to be my daddy.

Except the last night. Now, they had a dance every night after the bull riding. That last night after the bull riding, they were all going out there to put their horses up and come back to the dance. But them other guys on the square dance team, as soon as they got off them horses, they kidnapped my daddy and they made him go to the dance dressed as that woman. Well, he wasn't wanting to go and they was kind of scuffling around there. They kind of went to feeding him some of that Old Crow whiskey. After about four or five swallows of that Old Crow whiskey, my daddy said, "I guess I might as well accept this and just go on to the dance to see what happens." They did, and I'm going to told you they had one huge, large time. Some of them drunk cowboys was dancing with my daddy cuz they thought he was a woman. And he did things to them, pinch them here and there—stuff he really ought not to do—and it almost caused a fight. But then, all in the end, everybody had a great, great, large time.

6

HORSE-BREAKING LESSONS

THIS PARTICULAR RICH man lived in Dallas. He had six head of four-year-old, half thoroughbred ranch horses. He wanted my daddy to break them. My daddy broke horses back then and his whole life, really. But the man brought them over in an old bobtail truck and dumps the horses out in our arena. We ain't got no chutes. We ain't got no way to catch them. They ain't halter broke. My daddy saddles a horse, and he just goes to roping them things and they choke down. After they choke down two or three times, we put a halter on them. Daddy, he'd snub them up to that horse and I'd ease up there and go to fooling around trying to get a blanket on them, then ease around there and get them saddled. And he'd kind of pull them around here, there, and yonder. They're pulling back and all this, that, and the other.

Then when we get them saddled, I'd get on them things, and he'd lead me around with them. And everything's going pretty good, they're humping up, and I'm sitting in the middle of them. We get along on about three more of the horses. He ropes another one, and he chokes down. We get a halter on him, and get him snubbed to that horse. And I ease up there with a blanket and start to put the blanket on. Of course, that horse pulls back, and when he pulls back, he lunges forward, rearing up. And when he reared up, he's coming right at my daddy and the horse he's sitting on.

Well, his one foot goes over my daddy's horse's neck and his other front foot lands in the front of the saddle on my daddy. I'm standing there with that blanket, and that horse, he ain't getting off—just so happens to be standing on a part of my father in front of that saddle there that's not too awful comfortable. The horse won't get off. And finally, my daddy run his old finger into the horse's eyeball to get him off. The horse comes off. But when he drags that foot in that saddle across the front of my daddy, right about his belt buckle, it goes across something that I can't really, really say but I think that you can all imagine. And it hurt real bad.

Daddy turns the horse loose, he gets off his horse, and he pulls his britches down to look and see how bad he's hurt. I help him to the house. We put some ice on it and to make another long story short, there was not any more messing with them broncs for probably about two weeks until he healed up a little bit. When we did start messing with them broncs again, we kind of got them halter broke pretty good and the pulling back was over with before we went to try saddling them. We learned something about snubbing them horses. You really don't want to just rope one, snub him up right then; they need to be a little better halter broke before you go to trying that. And that still ain't a good way to do it, anyways.

7

HAVING NEIGHBOR TROUBLE

BUT WE WERE ALSO GETTING them broncs broke. They kind of skinned theirselves up a little bit here, there, and yonder, getting down on the ground and all that. We had an old gal with the humane society. Now, she'd come by, and she aggravated my poor daddy all the time about these horses being skinned up and us having all these broncs here, there, and yonder. She didn't like the way we was treating them broncs and treating other horses, and all this. We had another big steer pen about two miles from our house where we went down and roped steers. Well, that old gal, she had come by, seen my mother, and said she's coming back tomorrow—she's highly upset.

It happened to be a full moon that night. Me and my daddy, we thought, well, we don't want to mess with that crazy old woman, so we're just going to take them horses down there to our steer pen. They ain't even going to be here tomorrow. We tied them horses head to tail, which we did that a lot, and that's no big deal. But daddy's sitting on his good horse in the front, and I'm riding my horse in the back, holding that last one at the back. And here we go, a couple of miles—head to tail. This is all in the moonlight after dark, but you can see pretty good. We get down there to our little place and we ride up to a little old barbwire gate. My daddy gets off, opens it up, throws it out of the way, and he leads them horses through that gate. They kind of make a little circle out there but when that last horse went through, something scared him. He jerked loose from me and took off running. And he threaded the needle—run right between all them horses. Let me tell you something, in the moonlight, there was the dad-blamedest wreck going on. There was horses upside down, squealing, kicking, pawing, farting. I mean, it was a wreck for about ten minutes till everything finally got still. Finally.

We went to trying to get them untangled. It was the biggest mess—horses on top of each other. The only way we could get it done is just go to taking our pocket knives and just cutting halters off to get them loose. And that's how we got them loose. We messed around there and figured out that maybe doing things in the moonlight ain't really a very good thing to do. We abandoned that idea.

8

WILD CATTLE CATCHIN'

WE FOOLED around catching a lot of cattle, wild cattle. We had dogs, pit bull dogs, and them pit bulls, they did a wonderful, wonderful job for us. We could go out there in a pasture and find them cattle, usually some old thing that jumped out of the lot or kept getting out all the time. When we caught them, the people who owned them, all wanted us to just take them to the sale barn. So we moved around there and did that a whole lot.

We had stock frames on our pickup. You could haul horses in there. We'd haul them two horses in the back of the pickup all the time. We also had a real nice, open top, single axle, old trailer. You could put two horses in that thing too, which came out real handy. We could go out there and catch some old crazy bull or cow or something like that, load that thing in the back of the pickup with them tall stock frames, then hook the trailer up, put our two horses in there, and go home or go to the sale barn with it. All that and still we'd have room for our dogs and horses in the trailer.

A man called one day and had a red, bald-faced, horned Brahman cow to catch. We go out there in the pasture, and we sic them dogs on that cow. They grabbed a holt of her. One of them always grabbed the nose and the other grabbed the ear. You could leave them dogs on something or other for about ten minutes, and they'd usually just anchor it. I pulled out there in the pickup, Daddy's on his horse. And I know this sounds farfetched, but a lot of times I could pull up there to whatever them dogs had caught, get out, open the tailgate of the stock frames, and Daddy would call them dogs off. A lot of times them things would just jump up in that pickup, trying to get away from them dogs. That's what this thing did.

I closed the gate and we fooled around there so the thing wouldn't try to jump out of them six-foot-tall stock frames. Daddy put a rope around that old thing's horns—the horns was about three-foot long on that cow. He tied her head right there. We hooked up the trailer and loaded our horses, and off we go to downtown Cowtown—the stockyards at Fort Worth. That's the only place you could sell cattle at that particular time, as this was in the early days of the 1950s.

We get right there where you turn in to go to Billy Bob's. Of course, it's hot and my old daddy, he smoked them old cigarettes. It is so hot we had our heads hanging out the window. But he got $100 for catching that crazy old cow and he was thrilled because the whole trip hadn't taken two hours. Just as we turned the corner—right where Billy Bob's is today—to go unload at them stock pens up there, Northside, all at once, one of them blasted horns come right through the back glass of that pickup truck.

She was slinging the glass from the steering wheel over to the passenger side. Let me tell you something, we had our heads sticking out them windows because them horns was coming right close to us. She ripped that whole back glass out of that cab. We jumped out of that truck with it still running and it hit a curb over there and stopped. But daddy, he was sure teed off because I'm sure way back then, probably a pickup glass cost $25. But it had got mighty crowded in a hurry in the seat of that pickup. That's just one tale of us catching some wild cattle. But that ain't no bad tale—that's a pretty good one.

9

STAMPEDE DOWNTOWN

NORTHSIDE ... there are several stories about Northside. Years later, I was down there where the police barns are now. Behind Windy Ryon's old western store, they had an outside arena. We all go down there one night to rope steers—team rope a little bit. And we're sitting down there at that arena and it's Saturday night. There's a big crowd at Northside Fort Worth, down there on them streets—everybody running around them bars and stuff. A barrel race is going on in the arena, the team roping is right after the barrel race, and then they're going to have the bull riding.

There's probably twelve to fifteen of us horseback, all us team ropers sitting there on our horses. All at once, we all look up and somebody had left the gate open. There's about six of them rodeo bulls coming out of that pen, headed towards Northside ... downtown Northside. They got out.

The pickup men, they run out and take off after them bulls. About five or six of us cowboys take off after them also. They go right down there in front of the Cattleman's Steakhouse and in front of Leddy's right there. That's a little intersection. Two of them headed one way, and about two or three of them headed another way. There was one of them that headed up the hill from Leddy's. I take off after him.

These other cowboys, they take off after them other bulls to get them roped and get them penned—just get them off the brick streets. All them downtown people were scattering all over the place. Cars were pulling over. One of them bumped into another one. It's a little entertaining down there right about this time.

I follow that one up the hill and there's a policeman in a squad car there. He went to following that bull also. We get up there by the top of that hill and there's still a little old vacant lot to this day and a telephone pole there in the middle of that lot. I rope that bull and that cop gets out of the car and he is so stirred up—he is nervous. He don't know what in the world to do. "What are we going to do with this bull? What are we going to do now? I don't know what to do with him. I'm scared to death of cattle." And that bull, he ain't trying to do nothing. He's just sitting there on the end of the rope.

I said, "I'm going to ease him off over here and I'm going to tie him to this here telephone pole. You're going to go back down yonder to the rodeo arena and I'm just gonna sit here and wait. You tell some of them cowboys to

Stampede downtown

bring a gooseneck up here and when they get up here, then we'll just load him up." That's what we did. It wasn't no big deal, but it caused quite a ruckus downtown. And thank goodness nobody got runned over by one of them bulls or hurt really bad.

10

HORSES DON'T SHOP GOOD

THAT'S JUST one story about Northside. There's lots of wild stories there. Leddy Brothers is down there, and they built saddles. Great saddles. My old daddy, he had a saddle made and the tree in the saddle was guaranteed for life. One day we'd been out catching some cattle and someone called to come rope this bull. My daddy broke the tree in his saddle. He had this saddle made, broke the tree in it, and he called old Leddy up. He said, "Yeah, bring it down here. We'll replace the tree in it and it'll be just fine."

Daddy takes it down there. Leddy says it's going to be about a month when you get your saddle back. They got his saddle all fixed and they called. Daddy said, "Well, I'm coming through there Saturday and we'll fool around there, and I'll pick it up."

We get down there. Daddy's on his way to a calf-roping that Saturday, and he's got his roping horse in there—a nice, gentle, ol' roping horse. We pull up there in front of the store, he gets out, and we're talking about this, that, and the other. And old James Leddy, he said, "You know, we oughta just throw this new tree on your horse's back, being as you got him with you, and make sure it fits his back just right." Daddy said, "Yeah, that's a good idea. But I don't want to unload him right out there on that brick street. It's on a slant there, and he's liable to slip down." He said, "I'll pull up here at the top of the hill."

We're gonna have to carry that saddle plumb to the top of the hill. Mr. Leddy, he says, "It's too bad you can't just bring him in the store right there." And Daddy said, "Yeah, I can do that. I'll unload him, bring him right in here."

They laugh, and we go ahead and get him. It's Saturday at 11 o'clock and there is people everywhere. I mean, people is everywhere! We go up there and park, get that horse out and lead him down the street. And of course, people are looking, gathering around, wondering what's going on. We lead him right inside that store. And, man, there's people gathered around, there's people taking pictures, and they think that's something else. That horse, he didn't care.

We got him in that store and he was standing there and we throw that saddle on him, on his back. There's clothes racks and all kinds of clothes and boots and everything in the world in that western store where we were at. And that floor is pretty slick. We didn't think about this before, but every time you saddled that horse, he would relieve himself—take a dump. He sure enough did that time.

When he did, we were going to lead him up out of it. But when we got a hold of the lead rope there, he took a step back, and when he took a step back, his back leg slipped out from under him and he went to falling. Let me tell you, he was a-falling. I mean, he was scattering clothes all over that store—slinging brand-new clothes and clothes racks everywhere. He finally was laying flat on his side, and he couldn't get up. We had to get a bunch of new horse blankets and put them underneath that horse so he had some traction to get up.

But old Leddy, he didn't care. It didn't bother him a bit. He is laughing the whole time. I don't know how many clothes that horse messed up, but he thought it was quite a publicity deal because there was people all over that store taking pictures, talking about it, and looking at it. It was quite a scene there for Mr. Leddy and his little western store.

11

I DON'T LIKE ANTS

The first time I ever went to Stamford, out there at that rodeo, I was about eight years old. I made my first money right there at the rodeo. I got $8 a day running cattle out of the arena—the roping calves, double mugging yearlings, and milking cows. I rode down four horses a day. People would bring me horses to ride, and we'd run them things out of the arena.

We had our camp up there on the hill—a little two-horse trailer with a tarp off each side of it and a little rope pen for them horses. After the rodeo was over with that first night, we go up there and unsaddle the horses. I had to use the restroom. We had poured gasoline on all the red ant beds around there when we first got there that day, that morning. Well, I went around the other side of that trailer to use the restroom and we didn't see one of them red ant beds. I just happened to be right over the top of it and didn't know it.

Here in just a minute there's one red ant that stung me. And here, another red ant stung me. And here, another red ant stung me. And all of a sudden there was a mess of them stinging me. I was a-hooping and a-hollering and a-dancing around over there. Daddy come around and I told him them ants were in me. He yanked them boots off, pulled my britches off, and he went to whooping red ants off me. Let me tell you I had a mess of them stings on me. He had to get some alky-hol off somebody and rub me all down with that stuff. And that was a bad, miserable night right there.

12

LET'S WALK

Daddy used to buy old bucking horses that quit bucking, cause they was cheap. We purchased this one saddle bronc off one old boy down there at Mansfield. He run the Cowbell Rodeo. This old horse, he's a good-looking horse, and we thought we'd make a steer horse out of him. He had a big JD branded on his shoulder. He'd come out of Oklahoma, up there off of a ranch. He's bucking everybody off up there. But when they stuck him in that saddle bronc riding deal, they said when them cowboys went to riding and spurring on him, well, he quit bucking. That got all the buck out of him.

That boy that had the rodeo company, he didn't need him no more. So Daddy, he buys him and is gonna make a steer horse out of him and we bring him home. He is broke. You could turn him around, back him up and all that, and you could even rope something on him. He'd just gone to bucking them cowboys off in Oklahoma. We rode old JD—that's what we called him –down there to that old steer pen. JD did not want to walk. He would just prance sideways, this way and that way, and act stupid like that.

He just wouldn't settle down and walk down there, on that two-mile ride to that steer pen. It was sure aggravating to ride him like that. Daddy figured, I'll just fool around there and I'll just take my log and I'll just pull a log on him down there. He would walk like that, pulling that log. He'd pull that log down there and we'd rope on him and we'd pull that log back.

There was a road, a pretty busy highway, right there along the edge of a big field that we had to ride through. We messed around there, and Daddy fooled around, and he said, "I'm going to try something else on this horse to make him walk." He got his vise grip pliers out of the pickup and got on that horse. Sure enough, the horse went to walking sideways, prancing, acting stupid. Daddy reached up there and folded those ears over and clamped them vise grips on him. Man, his head went down, and he'd walk real nice that way. I mean, real nice, just so sweet. And we'd get down there, undone them vise grip pliers and roped on him. We thought he might have learned something. We started back home and Daddy tried to get them vise grips back on his ears and couldn't get them on his ears.

The horse wouldn't let him do it, so my daddy got off of him. He stood beside JD right there by his head and tried to reach up there and get that ear. And that horse went slinging his head. Slung his head right into my daddy's head, hit the side of his cheek, and knocked him down. That teed Daddy off pretty bad. He said, "Robert, give me a rope." He put his rope on JD's two front feet, and he said, "I want you to spur that horse and I want you to get this horse on the ground. I'll get them vise grips on him with him laying on the ground."

I got around there and I did all that. We had that rope on his two front feet, and I had the end of it. Well, that horse passed me running with his two front feet together. I don't know how the rope did not come off, but it didn't. And JD passed me. When he did, I turned off, and it did turn that horse upside down.

Here come Daddy—I will never forget—my daddy had that cigarette chomped down on and he is a-grinning. He looked like a mountain lion fixing to attack something or other. And he stuck them vise grips on that horse's ear. And we let that horse up. Daddy got back on him, and JD walked so nice. We got about halfway across that field and Daddy kind of got to feeling sorry for him, so he reached up there and took them vise grips off of him.

Well, he went to prancing again. That horse didn't learn nothing. We fool around there and my daddy thought he'd try something else. He had a little light jacket on, so he just got off and blindfolded that horse with his jacket. He got back on him and boy, he walked just nice and easy. Said, "Man, that worked real, real good."

We're going about halfway across that field and getting close to that highway on that little road. A friend of ours traded cattle all the time and he knew us real well—he's seen us riding. He pulled up there to stop and he's going to visit with us a little bit. And he had some sideboards on his old pickup, that he hauled stuff in. When we got up there getting pretty close to him, my Daddy gave him the sign to be real quiet and not say nothing.

He's got that blindfold on that horse and he's riding along there beside that pickup. He thought he'd ride him alongside that pickup frame and say *whoa* right before he got there. Well, he did that. He said, "Whoa," and that horse didn't stop of course—he must not have understood *whoa*. When that horse's head touched the side of that frame, he went absolutely berserk! He reared up and went to pawing. He tore the frames on that pickup all up. Bent the fender up! My daddy stepped off of him and that horse fell backwards—fell almost under that pickup. And he was a-kicking under there—kicking the underside and kicking the fenders of that pickup.

That was the dang-dest wreck you'd ever seen. Cars were stopped here, there, and everywhere—looking at this wreck going on. Of course, the little wreck didn't last too long. But that ol' boy who owned that pickup was hollering to get that horse out from under the pickup. It tore the frame off of it, bent the fender all to pieces, and I don't know for sure what it cost Daddy—maybe like $350 to $400 or so—to redo that man's pickup. That horse still didn't learn nothing—you still had to blindfold him or he'd prance around all over everywhere!

13

SITTIN' AND THANKIN'

MY OLD DADDY was retired from the Dallas Fire Department. I think them firemen down there, back then, they had a lot of time on their hands to sit and think about things—about life and everything else. He thought about what to do to a horse, how to get by him, and lots of other things. One day, we had to go over and load a horse for a customer—a colt that never had been loaded before. All we had at that time was a little old two-horse, side-by-side trailer. We get over there and of course, there ain't nobody home.

We catch the little ol' colt and back that trailer up against a fence—a good fence, not a barb wire fence. We back up in a corner and run a rope up through the front of that trailer and I held it back there out behind. The horse couldn't go around the trailer because of the fence, and he couldn't back up very far because he was in a corner. I'm sitting there, holding the rope, and old Daddy, he's smoking on one of them Lucky Strike or Camel cigarettes. When the little horse's head is about a foot from the back of the trailer, and I'm holding the rope, I said, "You want me to get something to kinda tap him on the rear end?"

He said, "No, just wait just a minute. Let's wait on him a little bit." He's smoking on that cigarette and here, in just a little bit, that colt—he's looking around in front of that trailer—and all of a sudden, he wants to go to the bathroom. He raised his tail up and he took him a little dump back there. If you've ever seen a horse do that, when they get through doing that, their rectum, it kind of looks like it's turned wrong side out and then they suck it back in.

Well, my daddy's standing there and he's smoking that cigarette. He pulled a bunch of fire off that cigarette. When that horse got through with going, and he kinda stuck that rectum out, my daddy stuck that hot cigarette in his rear end—and it got sucked back in there.

I'm going to tell you right now that horse went to the front of that trailer at a high rate of speed. Before he knew what was going on, we slammed the door shut on him and we had the little horse loaded. We had a big laugh about that. That really ain't the way you ought to load a horse. But I guess that's what my daddy thought of while he was down there at that fire station. When we got the horse home and we unloaded him, he was just fine and dandy. We'd break him, train him, and all that, and of course, we taught him to load properly in a horse trailer.

14

SHOEING HORSES IS A DANGEROUS JOB

THEN THERE WAS the time that I was shoeing horses at a stable—a big stable with probably 150 head of horses there. I had a customer, a woman, and she had an Arabian horse that I put shoes on at that stable. She called me up one night and said she had bought a brand-spanking-new Arabian stallion—she was so proud of him—a show horse. She was going to show him in these Arabian horse shows, but she said that the horse needed shoeing. I said, "Okay. I'll be over in a couple of days and get him shod for you." I set it up whatever day during the week—I never did go there on the weekend, too many people around.

She met me there and as soon as I drove up, I was going to pull down the hallway of that barn, get him out, let her hold him, and let me shoe him. She said, "Before we get started, I just have got to show you my horse. My new horse, he's just beautiful. Just walk down here and look at him." That huge barn had a big wide hallway, and all the stalls were double doors where horses could stick their head out to look around. That was a bad deal because people leading their horse right by them were liable to get horse-bit and have their horse run over them. But anyway, all them horses had their heads sticking out them stalls and all that.

We go down there. She puts a halter on him and she's still got him in the stall. He's got his head stuck out there and she's loving on that horse, talking to me about his breeding, petting on him. And I'm just standing there, kind of in front of them and she just goes on about how she fell in love with this horse and telling me all of the shows she's going to take him to and all this, that, and the other.

This woman, she had some pretty good-sized boobs and she's got that horse all snuggled up, with her arm around his neck, petting, loving, and kissing on him. And holy mackerel … I never seen nothing like this before in my whole life! All at once, that horse reached and got one of them in his mouth. He slung that woman around in front of him and over against the wall of that barn. He ripped off her blouse and her bra. And he bit off half of one of them boobs! I'm telling you what, afterward that woman is sitting on the floor, leaned up against that stall, and her blouse is in the hallway. Her bra is there too—and half of that boob is in that bra.

I ain't never seen me nothing like this before in my entire life. I'm about eighteen years old and I'm thinking, "Holy mackerel, it isn't even hardly bleeding—just a little bit!" But I saw that woman is in shock. I run down and I get my pickup and I get her purse out of her car. I drive down there and I literally have to pick her up—she couldn't even get up and walk. I picked her up and set her in the front seat—the only seat. Once I set her in the front seat of that truck, I got that bra and that piece that was in the bra. And, man, I booked it to the hospital with her.

The hospital was maybe a twenty-minute drive away, and I pulled up at that emergency room and there was two nurses walking out of that door. I hollered at them nurses. I said, "I got to have some help over here right now, right quick!" And here they come. They saw what had happened and I told one of them to get a wheelchair. They brought that and they unloaded that woman, got her in that wheelchair, and took her to the emergency room.

I got her purse and walked in. That girl behind the desk, I told her all what had happened and everything. She was asking all kinds of questions and we looked through that gal's purse and got her full name, phone number, and information. We found her husband's phone number on something, so I called him up. He worked about, oh, maybe thirty minutes away from that hospital. I called him up. I said, "Don't kill yourself getting over here because they got her in there treating her right now." He got there, I saw him, and I told him exactly what all had happened. I told him, "Looks like y'all got this handled so I'm going to leave." And he says, "Thank you very much for taking care of my wife. We'll be back in touch with you."

I left. She called later on that night, thanking me again. And I asked, "Do you think that I need to still come and shoe that horse later on when you get healed up?" She and her husband, who was standing there beside her, both said, "NO! That horse will be FOR SALE!" I never saw the horse again.

When I went back to shoe her other horse, about four weeks later, she was there. She looked all fine and dandy. The age I'm at right now, I probably would have had to ask—I would sure like to see what them look like now. I don't know whether they put a fake one on there or exactly what happened. But I was too young and too embarrassed to ask her. I never did know. But she looked perfectly normal.

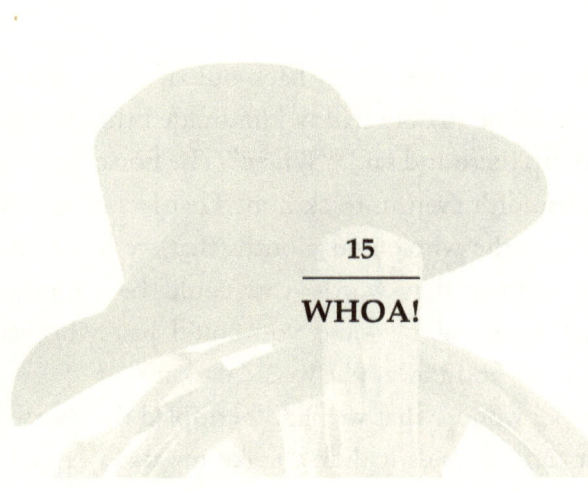

15

WHOA!

WE ALWAYS WANTED them horses to learn how to *whoa* when the command "Whoa," was said. Well, we had a horse that wouldn't—I don't know whether he was too dumb or what. But anyhow, down where we kept our steer pen, there was a creek, an old, dry creek that run through that place. It had a real steep bank on it, about fifteen foot deep. There wasn't no water there. Old Daddy and me, we rode and rode, and found us a place just right along that old creek where there was a limb that came out just right on the top of that creek bank. He took his jacket off and put it on that horse's eyes. He rode along there and reached up there and grabbed that limb and said, "Whoa!" Horse didn't whoa, and down that creek he fell—down there to the bottom.

I go down there with my horse and get him. Take that blindfold off of him. Lead him out of there. Daddy done it again—horse didn't whoa, down to the bottom of that thing he fell again. I bring him back out of there again. And the third time my old daddy blindfolded that horse, he rode him up there and said, "Whoa!" The horse froze. I mean, you couldn't even untrack him. That lesson stayed with that horse the whole two months that we had him. You could whisper that word—you could be a-loping along or a-running along—and you could just whisper that word, *whoa*, and I mean, he would park it!

Now, it's a wonder that we hadn't crippled that horse, but at that time, I guess it didn't make my daddy much difference. The horse learned the word *whoa,* but there's probably a better way to teach a horse that.

16

UNCLE SAM

I GOT DRAFTED in the army and they made a MP out of me—not by my choosing—that's just what they said they was gonna do to me. And they did. I wound up stationed right down there at Fort Hood, Texas. Well, off the base about five miles, I run into an old boy. He and his old daddy, they run cattle out there on that Fort Hood reservation. We became good friends. They had an arena and that old boy, he roped. He wanted me to bring my horse down there and rope with him at the South Texas rodeo. We practiced and all that, since he had a nice arena. We was roping calves, team-tying steers, double mugging, cow milking, all that stuff.

We're at the rodeo one night, watching a barrel race. We're back there fixing to team rope, all us team ropers were sitting back there. And this one old gal—I didn't know who she was—but this guy I was with, he sort of knew her a little bit. She come in the arena and made a barrel run on this horse. And when she came back through that alley, that horse was running wide open, just like they do. But he went plumb out of sight, out there in the dark, through the trailers and the trucks. Nobody knew where she, or that horse, went. They was calling our names out to team rope, so we went and team roped.

When the team roping is over with, we had won a little money. We had to wait for the bull riding to get over with to get paid. We're back there at the trailer and, lo and behold, here comes that woman on that horse from out of the dark. She comes riding by and my buddy there said, "Dang, you have a nice trail ride back there?" He kinda smarted off.

She said, "I'm done riding this horse. That scared me plumb to death. That's two or three times he's run off with me like that, and I can't stop him. Ain't no way I can stop him." We asked if she was alright, and she said, "Yeah, everything's fine. But ... it scared me to death."

My buddy said, "You ought to try to get that horse to stop, change some bits on him." She said, "I've done everything. I can't get him to stop. When he comes through that alley, he is off running and I can't get him whoa-ed."

She rides on by and I told my buddy, I said, "You got a real good arena. You could probably make that horse stop there at your house. I remember your roping boxes, and you got a little alley there. I know how you could probably get him to stop. Of course, you may kill the horse or cripple him ...," but I said, "if you want to go talk to that gal about it." He said, "What do you mean?"

I told him, "You could take that horse, you could get your lariat rope. Tie that lariat rope around the throat latch of that horse with a string where it can't work its way back down." And then I said, "You got them telephone poles sticking up about foot and a half up above your chutes. Go make a barrel run on him, come back through there. And when he comes through that alley, you could rope one of them posts and say, *Whoa!* about the time he hit the end of it."

He said, "You're crazy. I ain't gonna do that. That'll kill me." And I said, "No, it won't. It'll just kind of sling you out there on the ground. When you hit on that ground, roll a little bit and it won't hurt quite so bad." And he said, "Nah, I ain't going to do it!" I talked him into doing it. Said, "Bet you could get $300—she'll probably give you $300! And don't tell her how we're going to make him whoa ... just say there's a good chance we might cripple the horse or kill him."

He thinks about it, and I go up there to get our money that we had won, come back to the truck, and we're loading the horses. He said, "She's going to bring me that horse." I said, "Well, okay. Good deal."

She brings that horse a couple of days later to his place and she leaves. We get it all rigged up, put that rope around that horse's throat latch, tied up there with that string. I go set some barrels up out there in the arena. I told my buddy, I said, "When you come back through that alley and rope that post, don't forget to say, 'Whoa!' to that horse when he hits end of the rope."

Here we go. He comes in, makes a heck of a barrel run, comes back through that alley. He ropes one of them posts, and that horse is a-flying and, of course, it jerked that horse just almost right straight over backwards. And my buddy, he flew out there about fifteen foot and hit on that ground. He did roll, but it skinned him up a little bit. The horse is laying there, and we go over and kick the horse up. He's alright. We walked him around, and everything's fine and dandy.

I said, "Looks like everything's in pretty good shape. Get back on and go make you another run. Come back through there again." He said, "WHAT?!?!" I said, "Yeah, you got to see if it worked or not." I finally got him back on there, and here he come again. He made him another run. He roped that post and said, "*Whoa!*" And I'm going to tell you right now, that horse drawed eleven in that dirt —he stopped on his hocks! That word *whoa* got through to that horse right quick. He petted him, went back, made another run on him, come back through that alley, hollered, "*Whoa!*" and he did bury up. He buried up like one of them reining horses, stopping on his rear end. I said, "You might as well call that old gal up and tell her to come get him. He's ready to go home."

He did and she come got that horse and she got on him. The barrels was still set up in the arena and he told her, said, "Go make a run, but when you come back through that alley, holler *Whoa!* and you better be sitting down, because he's going to stop!" And he did. Those two did all that, and that woman was tickled plumb to death with that horse. She loaded him up and left.

It wasn't but probably about a month later that I got out of the army, and I come back home. I didn't go back to none of them South Texas rodeos. I don't know whether that stayed with that horse or whether it didn't stay with that horse, but I know one thing—it had him fixed for that particular time! But it's a little Western— might have hurt my buddy or killed him or whatever –all I know is that he took a pretty good wreck. But it dang sure worked. You might try it if your horse won't *whoa* very good.

17

MONKEY RUNNING BARRELS

RCA Rodeo is one of them other South Texas rodeos. We was in the rodeo. All us team ropers are sitting there in the back and they are having the barrel race. The team roping is right after the barrel race, and the roping chutes are plumb at the other end of the rodeo arena. There's two rodeo clowns there, one is out there in the arena, and they get the last barrel racer done. The clown gets out there and tells the announcer, "Whoa, whoa, whoa, whoa. Wait a minute. We've got one more barrel racer. This is the world champion barrel racer from such-and-such towns." And Lord-a-mercy, he's a-bragging on her! Said, "She just got here ... she was a little bit late entering, but she's here, and she has got one of the best horses in the world!" Just a-bragging, bragging, bragging. All that stuff, telling that rodeo announcer all that stuff.

It's a pretty long alley in that arena and we're back there. They had an Oldsmobile car parked right beside that alley. That's where the secretary was, she had the books, and everybody paid their entry fees there. But they just left that Oldsmobile there. This other clown comes by leading a Border Collie dog. And there is the cutest little monkey—a little spider monkey—sitting on that dog all saddled up. Got a saddle on that dog. And that monkey is strapped down on that saddle to that dog. He's got his little hat on. Got him a little fringe shirt on. Got him some chaps on. Got his boots on. And it is cute! We all get kind of tickled about that, just looking at that monkey.

That clown leads him about halfway down that alley. And when they announced this world champion barrel racer, that clown unsnaps the snap on that collar and that Border Collie dog, he goes out there and he is running wide open with that monkey on him. He makes the most perfect barrel racing run that you ever seen. When he turns that third barrel, that little old monkey, he's leaning on one side and sits back up in the middle and he turns that third barrel, and he is coming for home. I'm assuming he's running wide open.

I'm also assuming that the dog is supposed to stop at the clown in the alley. Well, the dog by-steps that clown in that alley. That clown makes a jump for him and he misses the dog. He don't get the dog caught. Here he comes right out that alley and comes right beside us. He runs under that Oldsmobile with that little old monkey on him. And I am not probably ten foot away from that monkey and that dog. I see that monkey's eyes are wide open. That monkey screeches, "Eee-eee-eee-eee," and I don't know what 'Oh Crap!' is in monkey language, but I think that's what it means.

All of a sudden, *splat!* Here comes that rodeo clown, and he's mad! He said, "Where'd that stupid dog go?" I said, "He's under that car." And he falls down there on his hands and knees, grabs that dog by the hind leg. He drags him out. That monkey is out—he is out like a light! He gets that monkey, unsnaps him from that dog. The monkey's lying on his back. Dog runs off. I don't know where that dog went, but that clown said, "Oh! My monkey—he's going to die! He's gonna be dead!"

He messed with the little monkey arms and wiggled him around, held him up, laid him back down. He puts his thumb on that monkey's chest like he's giving him a heart massage or something. And every time he'd mash on that little monkey's heart, those little ol' boots would just pop up in the air.

We're all dying laughing now. We feel sorry for the little ol' monkey, but we still don't know whether the monkey's dead or whether he's still alive or what. But he's still out like a light, I know that!

Well, they're calling our names out to rope steers, so we're all taking off down the arena to the other end of the arena—to the roping chutes. Me and my team roping partner, we're the first team up. And them RCA judges, they don't put up with no messing around. They want you to get in there, nod your head, and get out and all that. They got a rodeo to run. But all of us team ropers, every one of us is laughing—we can't hardly ride our horses—we are laughing hard about all this stuff. And them judges, they can't figure out what in the world all these idiot team ropers are doing laughing. Or what's so funny, because no one sees nothing funny. Me and my buddy, we ride in the chute, and we try real hard, real hard when we turn our horses around to get real serious about roping this steer and trying to win some money. Well ... it don't work—we miss our steer.

We ride on out the back. We can't wait to get out to the back of the arena to see if that little monkey made it or whether he didn't make it. But we can't find no monkey— we can't find no clowns—we can't find no nothing. I never did see that act no more and I never did see that clown no more. I don't know if the monkey made it. I don't know what they all did about that kind of stuff, but I hope the monkey got alright—that's all I can say.

18

COWBOYS IN A HURRY, NOT GOOD

I GET off the army base one night and we're supposed to be loaded up to get to a rodeo. I told my buddy that I'm going to be running late. Told him, "You have the trailer hooked up—it's a two-horse, side-by-side trailer—and have the horses standing there when I come across that cattle guard. We'll get them horses loaded and get gone. I'll change clothes in the pickup."

That all happens and I get out there. I come across that cattle guard, and my buddy has got them horses tied to the back of that trailer. His old horse has been loaded a jillion times before—mine too. He throws the lead rope over Ol' Dollar's neck. Ol' Dollar steps up in that trailer and gets about three-fourths of the way in there, but not all the way. He reaches across, gets that butt chain put across there, and here she comes flying out of there! She steps on his foot, and he don't know why she comes flying out of there, but he tries to load her again.

He's limping around there and tries to load her. She gets about halfway in there and flies out of there again. We got two cowboys here that are running late to the rodeo and we ain't got no time to mess with this horse that ought to load in the trailer anyways. My buddy, he hits her a couple of times with a lead rope and tells her to get in there, Dollar. She puts one foot in that trailer, and we hear this rattling, and up in the feed trough of that trailer, there was a rattlesnake. No wonder that horse came flying back out of there!

Then we felt so bad about him whooping Ol' Dollar two times with that lead rope because ain't no horse going to stay in a trailer with a rattlesnake. We killed the rattlesnake, and he had his old cow-catching trailer—an old flatbed, wore out pickup with an old gooseneck trailer. That's what we had to go to the rodeo in.

We make it—we go to the rodeo. But the next day when we tried to load Ol' Dollar back in that trailer, she ain't going to go. We had to pull that trailer out there in a lot—a little old lot—unhook the trailer and block the wheels up where it wouldn't move or nothing. And my buddy, he had to feed that horse at the back of that trailer, and it took probably three weeks before she finally would forget about that snake up in there and get herself up in the trailer. But it just goes to show you that two old, dumb cowboys in a hurry—usually when you're in a hurry—you usually mess up all the time.

19

SNAKES

I'M SHOEING horses down there at Coleman, Texas. A big ranch down there—they had about nineteen head of horses that I shod down there for them. Done that in two days: half of them one day, half of them the next. They had a little old barn there—kinda built out of standing-up crossties—that had a north wall on it. It's a perfect place. Pull in there in the lot, back up under an overhang there, catch a horse, and tie him up there. It's out of the north wind in the wintertime—and it's kinda nice, got a little sunshine coming in there, and then you got good shade in the summertime. Good place to shoe horses.

I'm down there one day and the foreman of that ranch and all the ranch hands, they're all gone in the pasture. They just leave me and half them horses standing there in a lot. I'd been down there and shoeing on them horses. I don't know, it's about two o'clock in the afternoon. My truck had been parked there all day and I'd taken a little

Snakes

old sandwich to eat there for lunch. I'd been there all day, till then, and I catch this old horse and I got him tied there where them crossties was standing up. He's gentle—all of them were gentle—so this one horse, I've got his front foot out on my little foot stand, clenching the nails, and my rear end is pointed toward the tailgate of my truck. And me and that old horse, we're right there—just standing there—with that old horse about to go to sleep while I'm clenching them nails.

All at once, crawling by my foot, going toward them crossties, right under that horse's nose, is a five-foot rattlesnake. And he ain't trying to bite me or coil up, he just trying to get to them crossties. He just comes crawling by, but it's about eight inches from my foot and I am deathly afraid of *any* snake. I see him and all at once, I just grab that horse around the neck and I'm trying to jump on that horse's neck and on his back.

It scares that horse to death, and he pulls back, and I fall off of him. And when I fall off him, on the ground, I'm fixing to try to crawl and get out of the way. I don't know where that dad-blamed snake has gone. And the horse steps on my hand with his back foot on them rocks and stuff. I roll over out of the way and I see about six inches of that rattlesnake's tail going in between them crossties. I jump up and I look around on the other side of them crossties to see if I can kill him.

Ah, but I don't know where he went. There was a pile of rocks back there. I guess that was his house. But I ain't got no idea how long or where that snake come from—if he'd come from out of the pasture. I don't know how long he'd been underneath my truck or nothing. But I know one thing, my hand was skint all to pieces and a-bleeding. I went over at the water trough and washed my hand up pretty good.

It took that horse about five minutes to settle back down with me petting on him. I finished that one foot on that horse. My hand was already swelling up and hurt, so I just loaded my stuff. I was planning on shoeing a couple of more of them horses before I left, but that wasn't going to happen now. My hand was swelling up and skint all to pieces. But there wasn't nothing broke because I could move all my fingers and everything. I just loaded all my stuff, turned that horse loose, left, and I went home.

Later on that night I'm sitting there watching TV. I got my hand soaking in a little bowl of turpentine—that takes the soreness out—at least I think it helps, pretty sure it does. My telephone rings and it's the foreman of that ranch. He's a good friend of mine—I've roped with him a lot. Well, he says, "Hey, I see where you shod. There was two of them horses that you didn't shoe that I left in that pen for you." And he said, "That one horse, he just had one foot shod and the other three wasn't shod." He said, "What in the world's the deal?"

I told him, I said, "Yeah, you're exactly right." And I said, "I'm going to tell you another little thing too. It's probably going to be about two weeks before I get back down there and finish them all up." I tell him what all happened with that snake and, oh, he thought that was so funny. But I didn't really think he was all that funny. Now why that snake didn't bite me, I don't know. I had been close to these dadblamed rattlesnakes many times before, and I guess the good Lord was looking out for me that I didn't get bit. He was looking out for me that day, for sure.

But a friend of mine at Abilene, we're like brothers—run cattle together, roped together, done everything together. We had a big rain out there in Abilene, flooded everything. Well, he calls me. He's got a big ranch and there's two highways that border his ranch. He had three water gaps along them highways. It's in March, still cool weather. You need a little jacket in the morning. He calls and said, "Bob, you need to come out here and help me in the morning. I got to at least get them water gaps fixed on the highways before them cattle get out and get hit by a car." He had fence washed out all over inside that ranch, but that didn't matter much. So, I go out there. I told him, "All right, I'll be out there." And I get out there just shortly after daylight.

He's got a little Jeep that he drives around—had a little trailer hooked onto it and had some posts and some wire. He's getting something out of it—I don't remember what he was getting—but I got out of the truck. He said, "Grab two or three of them steel posts and some stays right there and get that little post driver there and throw it in the back of that trailer." And I said, "I'll get this stuff and we'll be gone." I get that stuff and throw it in that trailer—the post driver, four or five posts, about that many cedar stays—and here we go.

We've gotta drive about, I don't know, four miles over there to this first water gap. We drive around over there and the water gap, it's pretty steep down there where that thing is. We pull off the road, kinda over in the ditch, and get out. He had him a brand spanking new pair of them waders like them fishermen wears, where you wade out there in the creek. He thought that's a great deal—thick waders where you can wade across that water and not get wet and all that stuff. He's getting them things on, and I look down there and it's probably 12-15 foot down there to that water gap. And I see that we're going to hafta have a steel post drove in the ground where one's washed out. I get a post and I throw it down there where we're going to have to drive that post in and I throw that post driver down there with it. Then I walk just about twenty foot there—where I can kinda shimmy down there—and I get down there and I pick that post up and I put that post driver over the top of that post and I hit that post—but it didn't feel just quite right.

I couldn't understand it, but anyhow, I didn't really think nothing of it. But when I picked that post driver up to come down and hit that dadblamed post again, there's about a three-foot rattlesnake fell out of that post driver, right on top of both of my boots. And I'm going to tell you right now, I left the scene. I screamed and I run. I assume that the first time that I'd done it—I still can't believe there was a snake in a post driver— the first time I hit that post I assume that I killed the snake. But I didn't realize that at the time. Let me told you what, I did run off now. My friend's looking at me like, *What in the world is the matter?* I told him, I said, "There's a stupid snake in your post driver." He said "What?" I said, "Yeah."

He comes down there with them brand spanking new waders on. He has to wade across that creek. He waded across that creek, he grabbed that water gap up—that barbwire water gap. He's bringing it across that creek, pulling it across there. And I'm driving that steel post in there where it belongs—without no snake in the stupid post driver—when about that time, he snags his wader with some barbwire and they go to filling up with water. That water is cold. He come out of there and he takes his waders off and his britches are wet. He says, "We fixed the water gap. But you know, we're going to get back in that Jeep and drive around. We're going back to the house, have a cup of coffee, and we've started off with a rattlesnake and a post driver, and I done tore up my new waders." I said, "This day ain't started out very good at all." We had a cup of coffee and got something to eat and then we went and fixed them other two water gaps.

But let me tell you, them snakes and me, we don't get along at all. One night, I go out there after shoeing horses all day, and me and him, we're going to rope. That evening, Dee's gonna come out there and we're going to cook supper and all that and have big time. We do that—I shoe them horses all day long. Me and him, we go down there and rope. Dee comes out there and his wife's down there at the arena. We're all having a big time. We're roping and his wife's riding a barrel horse around. It come time to quit, and we go up there and unsaddle. His wife had some supper fixed, so we ate supper.

Of course, it's plenty after dark. I got through eating and we're gonna go home. I got me a cup of coffee to go. I walk up to that door to walk outside—the porch light's on. Dee, my wife, she's right behind me. His wife's right behind her. I push that door open. I step out that door—and I'm looking down—I look down everywhere I go. When I stepped out that door looking down, I step across about a four-foot rattlesnake stretched out there right beside that dadblame door, right along that door. And I can't even talk, I jus throwed that coffee cup in there. Hot coffee went over me, my wife, and everybody else. I can't even talk and my wife said, "It must be a snake." And sure enough, he went to rattling.

They keep about three shotguns right behind that door. His wife got that shotgun and she blowed the hound outta that dadblamed snake—shot a little bit of the corner of the house off. But I almost had another heart attack.

Several years later, same place, we're gathering cattle and there's about seven, eight of us a-horseback. My buddy—it's hot in the summertime, early in the morning, but it's hot—he's got a straw hat and some sunglasses on. We got about, I don't know, forty cows going down the fence, fixing to go through a little twelve-foot gate. Everybody's right there like they're supposed to be. And my old buddy, he's coming down

Snakes

the fence and he's probably about sixty to seventy-five feet from me, he jumps off his horse and said, "I got to kill a snake!"

He's got some big old rocks. We can't go over there to look 'cause we got to hold these cows and they're going through that gate. He fools around there and he's taking some big, humongous rocks that are laying around everywhere and he's hitting that snake. He hits him and he uncoils, he coils back up and then he hits him again. He uncoils and coils back up again. He's a-rattling—he's mad. My buddy hits him four times with some big rocks, and it finally kills the snake. He picks that snake up and hangs him over the fence—a barbed wire fence. He's about a five-and-a-half footer.

He comes riding up—the cows are in the pen where we want 'em, got the gate closed—he comes riding up to me, hollering, "Man, that's the biggest snake I ever killed! That's the biggest snake I ever killed!" And I said, "What's that on your face?" And he just froze. He said, "What do you mean?" I said, "You got three white drops, looks like white milk, up above your glasses, between your hat and your glasses. And you got three or four of them same spots on your cheekbone."

He said, "Here, take my handkerchief and wipe it off." He didn't hardly move. And I said, "What is that?" And he said, "Well, Bob, I've never, ever heard of this before, but the second time that I hit that rattlesnake with a big rock, he coiled right back up and he reared back. And he spit something—like a spitting cobra—and it hit my sunglasses. I had to take my handkerchief and wipe my sunglasses off."

I said, "You didn't get it all off because you still got them drops above your eyebrow and on your cheek!" It scared him to death, and he said, "I've never heard of a snake ever doing that!" I said, "I never have either. Spitting cobra, yes, but not a rattlesnake." He said, "Well, he dang sure done it!"

I wiped that off, and I still don't know what it was. Venom, rattlesnake venom, looks like the color of urine, but this was white, solid white, milky looking stuff. I've asked several snake catchers about that, and ain't nobody ever even heard of a snake spitting anything like that. I don't know whether it was venom or I really ain't got no ide-y what it was. But I know one thing, if he hadn't had them sunglasses on, it would have went right in his eyeballs. And I don't know whether it was venom or what it was, but I don't think it would've done his eyes no good. I've never heard of a rattlesnake or any other snake, other than a spitting cobra, doing that.

Me and my wife, we go and check some cattle south of Abilene one evening late. Once we looked at all the cattle, it's about forty-five minutes before dark, and we decide we're coming back—we are done. I pull up to the steel gate and she gets out to open the gate. The broomweeds were real bad that year and I'm always scared of snakes down there—lots of them. I pull through that gate, and she closes the gate to come back up to that first step in that truck. We both see it just about the same time—about six foot off to the side of the front of that truck, there is a rattlesnake that stuck his head up above them broomweeds, like a foot-and-a-half up above them broomweeds.

Now, these broomweeds are almost three foot tall, and this snake's got his head up above them broomweeds, looking around, and we both said, "Holy mackerel!" And what this snake is doing—it's indescribable nearly—but this snake has got his body stretched out, laying on top of them broomweeds. Them broomweeds was thick, but they was holding him up, and all at once he just levitated —or just in midair—just came up and jumped like three foot and hit some more broomweeds. Then he did it again, and then he did it again, and he hit a little net wire fence right on the other side of my pickup. He did all that fast, and we couldn't believe what we had just seen in the first place. It was remarkable! I never knew a snake could even do something like that.

Most of the time I just shoot them snakes with a shotgun and leave them. But as big as he was and for what we had just seen him do, for some reason, I wanted his hide on a board. I got my shotgun—he was coiled up, and oh, he is mad—he's a-rattling. And I just let him get his head and about six, seven inches of his body off his coil, and I shot his head and that much off him and killed him. I had a long-handled shovel in the back of the truck, but I'm so scared of them snakes, I can't even touch one of them. So I asked Dee to take that shovel, pick him up with that shovel, and load him in the truck. He is big and so heavy she barely could get him loaded in the back of that truck. We load him up—well, she did. We drove to Abilene.

It's an hour after dark. I pulled up to an old chiropractor's house that I knew. He caught snakes down there every spring on that ranch, and I knocked on his door. He said, "What are you doing here?" I said, "Me and Dee, we killed us a snake. I want you to gut him and skin him. I want you to put his hide on a board for me." He run out there in his bare feet saying, "Where's he at?" Oh, he was awfully excited—he loves them! I told him that he's in the back of the truck. He reached over and got that thing. And that snake was about six-and-a-half, seven-foot long is what he was. He said, "I've never seen one this big ever on that ranch. I've never caught nothing like this!" And I told him what that snake had done, and he absolutely could not believe it—and it is very, very unbelievable!

But I'm desperately afraid of snakes—I don't want no part of them!

20

HORSE STUFF

I used to go help an ol' boy up in the town of Guthrie, Texas. He managed a big ranch up there. About a dozen of us cowboys would go up there every spring and every fall. We'd brand in the spring, gather them cattle in the fall, and sell the calves. There's some pretty wild ol' tales up there. We'd take about twelve of us cowboys and we'd get there and put the horses out there on the ranch. We'd spend the night at the hotel and restaurant in town. Then we'd get out there at daylight the next day and there we go—we'd take off. There were about twelve sections in that one big pasture—we'd ride along there and drop one ol' boy off, and in about half a mile drop another guy off.

I happened to ride a young horse up there and I wanted to ride him pretty hard, and I told the manager of that ranch—I said, "I want to take the long way around." He said that was fine. We all hit it at a trot, and we're all dropping this one off and that one off and another one off. I'm going all the way around that twelve-section pasture. Way on the backside of it, I knew there was a place that this young horse and I might have a little trouble getting him to go down this pretty steep bank. But I made it all right—with one exception. You had to go down this bank kind of at an angle. I'm riding down this little old trail, and at the bottom of that trail, it's probably about, oh, I don't know, about fifty feet down. There was a little washout place, about five or six-foot deep, and we are going to get down there alright.

But right as I went down on the trail at an angle, there was a cedar bush sticking out—just a little bit—in that trail about the size of a man's hat. And it's about head-high on a man that's riding a horse. I'm going along there, and I ride right by that cedar bush. My hat is about even with it, and all at once there's something that goes "Grr-grrr-grrrrr!" It scared me half to death, and it scared that horse—he jumped off that bank and jumped down in that washed out spot and went to bucking. I got him rode—got him pulled up. And I didn't know what in the world that dadblamed thing was. But I looked up there, and it just so happened that we had invaded a badger's home—and he was highly, highly upset with us! Well, I continue on around and we gathered the cattle. We did all the cattle work and all that kind of stuff.

Up there at Guthrie, there's some pretty wild, old country. Another time that I went up there, I was also on a young horse. There's about a dozen of us old guys. We had to go down a pretty steep little canyon, and there was three

Horse stuff

cow trails that came together, and they were about three-foot deep, them cow trails were. I thought I might have a little trouble with my horse getting them down there, so I let everybody go ahead of me. My buddy, he went ahead of me, and I started my horse right down there. I thought my horse would follow them other horses down that little trail.

I got about halfway down that little trail, and he decided to turn around and come back up to the top. Well, he jumped. I was into one cow trail and he jumped over into another cow trail. It's a wonder that he hadn't fell down—I don't know what kept his feet up. But he come back up at the top, and I went to pulling him around, trying to get him to go down that trail. I was having all kinds of trouble, and all them boys are down there laughing at me. I finally told my buddy, I said, "Get up here and help me, give me your rope." I put that rope around that horse's neck. And I said, "Now, you go down that trail and I'm gonna follow you. And if this horse don't go, you just dally up and you could lead him down there." We did all that and I started down that trail, and that horse, he stopped and he wouldn't go. That rope pulled up tight around his neck and I mean, he come down in about two big, long leaps.

My feet was up in the saddle. I don't know how I got him rode down that thing, but it was pretty wild. Everybody was laughing at me—and then I had trouble. I took that rope off his neck, and my horse was in love with my buddy's horse. I guess he thought that horse had done all that too. But I had a little trouble getting him to separate from that horse. But we made it all right.

I had a lot of good horses in my life, but I had a lot of sorry ones too. I had a bald face horse, a beautiful horse, come off racetrack. And I had been roping on him—he made a great roping horse. The only problem was sometime another—you never knew when it was going to happen—I think his brain would short out. You would liable to be on him, and he'd liable to just go to running backwards, shaking his head, and fall over backwards with you. I don't know why. I think he had a loose screw, as some might say. But he was such a beautiful horse and such a good horse when he didn't do that—that's why I kept riding him.

Up there at Guthrie, I'd take him up there. I'm dragging some calves on him to the branding fire. It's my turn to drag. I got on that horse, drug some calves—I'd drug up probably three calves on him—little roping sized calves, weighed about two-hundred pounds. He's doing a wonderful job. Cattle work is going great. I got my rope, I reached over there, and I roped a little ol' bitty baby calf—don't hardly weigh nothing. When I started pulling him—I was pulling him up there to the fire—and all at once, that horse, he just stopped, lowered his head and went to shaking his head, running backward, fell over backwards—just like he had done before. When he did, of course, it sure made me mad, but he didn't get on top of me, so I just tied him down right there. And it just so happened to be right in a gate.

Horse stuff

We went ahead with working the calves and he stayed tied down for maybe two hours till we got through. Whenever it was time to turn the cows out, the manager at the ranch said, "You need to untie your horse. We need to open the gate and let them cows out." I said, "Well, I don't even see no horse over there." I went over, and I opened that gate, and about two-hundred cows went out over the top of that horse. I thought that would fix that horse from then on—that he never would do that again. And it did for probably six months.

I took him to roping, roped on him and won money on him. Oh, he was just a wonderful horse. In Abilene, they had a little ol' roping there one time—a place called Old Abilene Town. It was kind of an old western town, little dude ranch kind of thing. It was a huge roping—people come from everywhere. It's right off the interstate. But the heeling box was just an alley, it didn't really have no box there. Heelers just stood their horse in that little alley, and you go rope. Me and my buddy—it's a four-head roping—we come back "high team back" in that roping. It's gonna pay some good money. People's everywhere, and my horse hadn't pulled that stunt on me in mighty long time.

I'm standing in that alley on our last steer and all we gotta do is catch this steer to win this roping. When them gates banged open, all at once, my horse, he turned around and ran off with me. Ran plumb off towards the interstate! Through some horses, through people, and I could not stop him. My buddy went out there and he roped the steer. He didn't know that the horse had even done that. He was looking around for me, when he turned that steer off. I finally got my horse stopped and turned around, and I come back through that alley—whooping his rear end—went down there and roped that steer. We still placed in the roping, but people was screaming and hollering and clapping and they thought it was all pretty funny. I didn't think it was so funny at the time!

After that, I shod horses for an old boy that sold horses out in California. And I told him about that horse, and I said, "Have you got a good spot to sell that horse just for a trail ride horse?" And he said, "I sure enough do."

I said, "You just send him out there and get him sold. And whatever you do, don't rope a steer on him because you're going to love him." But I said, "Some time or another, he's going to do that head shaking deal and fall over backwards on you." That's where that horse went—went to California, and I hope he made a nice parade horse, riding in the Rose Bowl. I don't have no idea what happened to him, but that was just one of the horses that didn't work out too good for me.

21

PETS DON'T NEED TO BE AROUND HORSESHOEING

I SHOD horses for a rich man there in Abilene—a banker. He had a place, right north Abilene, and another one up in Hamlin—up close to Aspermont. He had about seven horses in each one of them places—ranch horses that I shod. And I go up there to that place, and I'd been there several times. and he had an old, big, white gander goose that just hung around them horses all the time. You just had to catch them horses and just walk around him—and he'd spread his old wings out and kinda hiss at you. But he never did do nothing, he just got in the way. And I'd walk around him, shoe them horses and kinda push him outta the way.

I was shoeing on this one horse and this boy that was there with me, he looked around over there and he was asking me how I drive them nails in them horse's feet. I got that horse's front foot up, and he had his head stuck around there. He was bent over, and we didn't pay that goose no attention. But, I mean, that goose come up behind that feller and bit him on the back of the leg. He jumped into me, and I jumped into the horse, and the horse pulled back, and we both fell down, and the horse was still pulling back. And it was a pretty good little wreck there for a minute. It didn't hurt neither one of us, but that boy pulled his britches down and I mean blood was running out of the back of his leg. That goose got him real good!

I told him—he wiped the blood off and pulled his britches up—and I said, "Let me get my rope and I'm going to rope that goose. Maybe we'll get rid of him." I got my rope and he drove that goose around. He's walking around in front of my pickup, and I hid up there at the headlight, and that goose come around there, and I roped that goose. It settled right around where his neck comes out of his body. And when I roped him, that goose took off and went to flying. He looked like a kite on the end of that rope up there. Squawking and a-quacking and a-flopping around up there in the air. It was pretty funny. Then I jerked him back down, jerked him down on the ground. That old boy, he messed around there and took that rope off the goose. And that goose, he did leave us alone after that. He took off to the barn. Every time I come up there and shoe them horses by myself, that goose would be there when I'd drive up, and he'd leave. I never had no more problems with that goose.

22

GOAT SENSE

At that other boy's ranch up there in Hamlin, he had an old stinking Billy goat. Oh, he stunk bad! Had horns about foot-and-a-half long. He stayed with them horses all the time. I go up there and I'd shoe them horses. I'd pull into a lot—it had a little lean-to deal—a railroad car they made into a little barn, with a tack room and an overhang on it. I shod horses under there. And that Billy goat was kinda like that goose—he never bothered me—you just have to push him out of the way and walk around him. Wasn't no big deal.

One day I was up there, and that goat, he was a little bit more aggressive than what he usually was for some reason. I don't know why, but he was. I was beating on my anvil on that shoe, and I turned around and that goat was right there. He reared up like he's fixing to hit me with them horns. And when he did, I reached around behind me and got my big horseshoeing hammer, and I hit that goat right across where them horns come out of his head—hit him hard. He went back down and he made the funniest sight—he'd turn his head one way and turn it another way. He'd make the funniest little old growling sound. And he turned around—went to walking off—and well, he didn't walk too straight. He kinda walked a little bit on the crooked side—kinda like an old drunk. He went over in the corner of that lot and laid down. And I thought, *I might have killed that goat, but I don't know.* But he didn't bother me no more.

That night I called that boy down at that ranch that owned them horses and that goat. I told him, I said, "I might have killed your goat." And told him what happened. He said, "I'm going to tell you that I don't know why I got that goat. But the other day, I was saddling a horse, and I was walking around that goat, and I stepped out of that railroad car with a saddle, and that goat hit me right in the back. Knocked me down—nearly under that horse." He said, "I hope you did kill him!"

I didn't kill the goat. But every time I went back up there, that goat was just like that goose. When I'd pull in there with my truck in that lot, he'd go over there in that spot, and he'd lay down and he never did bother me no more.

23

BURNIN' BRUSH

MY BUDDY—WE partnered on a ranch down south of Abilene—he had a bulldozer. There was a lot of cedar down there on that ranch. And it used to be, back around 1944 or 1945, that they had an army camp there and the army camp owned that ranch. Down there, they had a lot of maneuvers, soldiers, and stuff down there. They shot tanks and all kinds of guns to get ready. They were trying to figure out how to get to invade Normandy Beach. They had different things built down there and they'd shoot them with them tanks, so there was shrapnel all over that ranch.

My buddy, he was pushing cedars—cedar will take a ranch plumb over if you don't do something with them. We had cedars piled up and I mean to tell you, just piled up everywhere! Big, humongous brush piles! We let them brush piles sit there for about a week to let the leaves kinda dry a little bit on them. All I had to do is go back down there and just take a little old cigarette lighter and just light a couple of them leaves up. Man, them cedars would take off to burning and I mean, they'd go—they'd burn! We had seven or eight of them great big ol' piles pushed up just here, there, and yonder—all pretty close together.

And my buddy, he is still running that dozer pushing cedar. And I was walking around there setting them things on fire to get rid of those brush piles. I'd set about half of them off, and I set another one and walked away from it about maybe sixty to seventy foot to this other brush pile. All at once, we had a big KABOOM! There was one of them old, old tank shells, out of one of them army tanks, that was still alive in there. He had pushed it up in that brush pile, and when that fire hit it, that thing blew up! It blowed fire about three-hundred foot up into the air. Brush everywhere. A big boom!

And I don't know why in the world that I did what I did, but I just hit the ground. My buddy just happened to be looking at me when all that took place. Oh, my God! He thought I was dead. He jumped off that dozer, come running over there. I wasn't dead, but it scared both of us about half to death!

Later on, he had some government money some way to push all that brush. Then the government man, he come down there, and he said, "I want you to push this cedar and just let it lay. Don't pile it up, just let it lay all over the ground." I don't know why—it's just like a typical government man—didn't know what he's doing. But it was a mess! I'd walk along there with a Para burner,

Burnin' brush

carrying one of them little old butane bottles, and I'd have to walk over them cedar limbs—carry that thing and walk and set them things afire. There wasn't even a brush pile no more, just stuff laying all over the ground.

I did it all one day, and I'm going to tell you, I was about to give out, stepping over them limbs and carrying that old butane and all that. The next day, we come back down there. I had my little ol' Jake—my little old wild-cow working horse that I used. That's all he was worth a hoot for, but he'd run over rocks and everything in the world. I just used him for gathering cattle. He'd buck every time he saddled him, but once the buck was over with, then you could ride him, rope on him, do whatever you wanted to. I carried him off down there, unloaded him and tied him to the trailer. I pulled some of them limbs up there and set them afire, kinda behind him to see if that was going to bother him. Didn't bother him a bit in the world.

I took that butane bottle, and I hung it on that saddle horn. I got on him and I'm riding along there, and he's the one that's stepping over all them limbs and stuff, and I'm burning brush, and boy, we're doing really, really good. My buddy—once again he's on that dozer—he's pushing or knocking down some more cedar trees. He ain't very far away from me, pretty close. And I'm doing this for about forty-five minutes. I don't know what happened, unless as that butane bottle burned down, it got condensation around the outside of it, and it's kinda cold. I guess that cold was down on that horse's shoulder and for whatever reason, I do not know why, but he went to bucking. And

I've got that butane bottle up there by my leg and I got that Para burner—fire is coming out of the end of it—and he's a-bucking and going across all them cedar limbs. I don't know how he stood up and didn't fall with me, and some way or another, I'm getting him rode—because I ain't no bronc rider anyways—but I'm getting the horse rode.

I've got that Para burner up in the air, and my buddy, he's looking over there and he's watching all this—and he said that it looked like a big torch up there in the air. I can't get that horse's head pulled up to make him quit bucking. But being as I'm getting along all right and he ain't got me bucked off, I kinda got with him pretty good, and I just took that Para burner—he had his head down—and I just blistered between his ears with that fire and that made him quit bucking. I got him pulled up and he stopped all that and everything's fine and dandy. And my buddy, he's laughing over there and he said, "You wanna try that again?" I said, "I'm going to take that extra butane bottle with me and I'm going to hang it on the other side. Maybe that's what was wrong. We had just one butane bottle and he wasn't even and maybe that was what was the matter with him." So, that's what I done and everything was just fine and dandy. We burnt brush for two days down there that way and got a lot of brush burnt. But that might have not worked out quite so good.

24

TRYING TO FIX OL' SPOILT HORSES IS INTERESTIN'

MY OLD DADDY—MY daddy was a great cowboy and a great horse trainer, way better than me—but sometimes, some of his ideas didn't work out too good. We had a place leased and had some cows on it. Had about twenty-five to thirty cows on this place. We lost the lease on it and couldn't find another, so we just had to take them to the sale barn and sell them. We'd had that place and them cows for, I don't know, three or four years. There was always an old white Brahman cow with horns and she never, ever came in a lot ... *ever!* We'd feed all them in a lot, and every one of them would come in just great. But she never would—she'd just stay out there all the time. When she'd have a calf, she'd keep her calf out there, and then we'd have to get that calf trapped to get him sold.

But we had to get all them cows off that place. There was an old brushy creek, kind of a dry creek, went through that place. We're going to saddle up and go down there and get them cows penned. Get some guys down there to help haul the cows to the sale and all that. For us, we had just got in a horse we were going to train for a guy, and he was an old spoilt thing. And my daddy said, "I'll just ride him. I know you could rope something on him, but he is pretty sorry."

I told him, "Daddy, don't ride that horse. Catch one of our good horses, go with me. You know we're gonna have trouble. We're going to have to rope that old crazy cow. They won't come in a lot. We've got to catch her. It takes a pretty good horse to do that."

He said, "Aw, this old horse, he'll be all right. Don't worry about it. We'll work it out all right." We get down there and we pen all of them with some cake sacks and stuff. And sure enough, that old white Brahman cow, she stood off out there. In the first place, Daddy went to try and bridle that horse. The bridle was in the back of the pickup. He went to try to put the bridle on him, and that horse was slinging his head and wouldn't let him get the bridle over his ears. He slung his head into my daddy and just about knocked him down, and of course, that upset him pretty bad. I don't know why, but my daddy could take that horseshoeing hammer, and he could tap a horse between the eyes and drop him—just knock him plumb out. Usually, a horse would get up from that deal and he was a different horse.

Daddy reached in the back of that truck, and he took that horseshoeing hammer, and he tapped that horse between his eyes. And that horse, when he fell, he flopped

Trying to fix ol' spoilt horses is interestin'

around there, and his legs was almost underneath the truck, and he is a-scrambling around there—kicking and flouncing—trying to get up. He kicked the side of the truck, kicked the fenders, kicked the gas tank—it was a wonder it hadn't blowed up—he knocked a hole in it and gas going everywhere. My daddy had been a-smoking, but thank goodness, that horse knocked the cigarette out of his mouth. It was a wonder it hadn't blown all of us up. It was a heck of a wreck there.

Directly that horse, he finally flopped around, got his feet out from under that truck, and got up. That did fix him, my daddy just stuck that bridle on him. He put his head in that bridle and wasn't no problem whatsoever.

My daddy gets on him and here we go. We take off and that cow, she'd done run off down there in that old dry creek, all brushed up, and the rest of the pasture was open. Daddy said, "You stay out here in the open. I'm gonna ride down that creek. I'll push that old cow out of that brush. She'll come out there in the open, and when she does, you can rope her."

I said, "Well, all right. But ... when you push that cow out of there, come on out there with her. Because when I rope her, I might need a little help. She's going to want to fight the rope on her. You can get another rope on her and we'll heel her. Get her down and then go get the truck and trailer, and we'll load her."

He thought that was a good plan. Sure enough, I'm riding along there waiting right along the edge of that creek, and he pushes that cow out there to me. I take off after her and I rope her, but I don't know where my daddy's at—I have lost sight of him. I know where he was, but not now. Of course, she's wanting to fight, and I laid about two trips on her. On the third trip, she laid down, I got off and I tied her down—tied two feet on her and got her tied down. And just about then, my daddy, he come riding up there. He didn't have no cap on his head. Had a tree limb stuck through the breast collar of his horse. He was skint up, and his shirt was tore about half off. I said, "What in the world happened to you?" and "Where have you been?"

He said, "When that cow come out of there, I had to trot up to bring her on out of that brush. And when I did, that horse run off with me, down that creek—that dry creek bed—and we was going through that brush and I couldn't stop him. I was ducking and diving them limbs, tore my shirt up, and everything in the world. Finally, when we got to the fence, he just stopped."

I said, "Yeah that's about just what I figured that idiot would do!" Well, my daddy was just skint up a little bit, cut up a little bit from some tree limbs when they tore his shirt off, and had four or five scratches on his ol' body.

We got the cow tied down, and we go up there—and of course—we didn't think about that horse tearing that gas tank up on that truck. We didn't have no gas, it wouldn't start, so we couldn't load her. Had to wait around there. And directly, about three of them ol' boys showed up with their truck and trailer to haul them cows to the sale. They loaded their trailer with the cows in the

Trying to fix ol' spoilt horses is interestin'

pen, and we took another trailer down there and got that stupid cow loaded so she could go to sale too. We had to get a wrecker to come down there and get our pickup, take it to the mechanic, and get another gas tank put on it and get the fenders all fixed up. I don't remember how much money that cost, but that wasn't such a great idea that my daddy had about riding that stupid horse down there, when we could have just rode a real good one down there. Most things worked out pretty good that he'd come up with—just that particular time—it didn't work out so good.

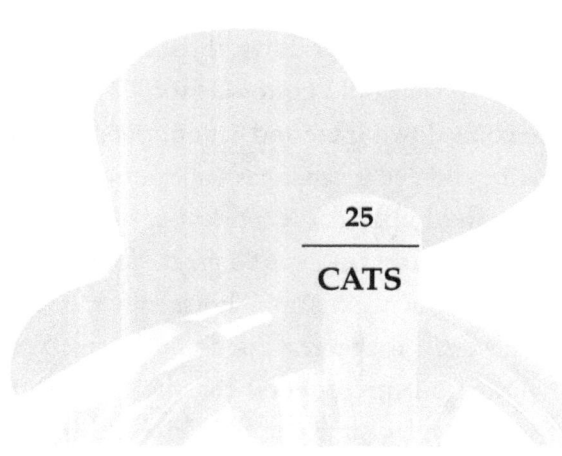

25

CATS

Around the barn, I had two old yellow cats. Sometimes cats don't do very good around horses. I had little problems with them things getting hurt a few times. But I lived right on a major four-lane highway, and there wasn't no fence there in front of my barn. You could ride right up to the road. One day I had come in from shoeing horses and I was gonna saddle these horses up and go rope. I had hay stacked in that barn, an alleyway and a ten-stall barn there. I walked down there to catch me a horse. About halfway down that barn, I happened to see one of them old yellow cats sitting on top of that hay. There's mesquite trees out in front of that barn, a bunch of them.

I didn't pay no attention to that old yellow cat ... didn't even think about him. I go down there, and I catch me a horse. I'm leading him down that little alley—that narrow alley—it wasn't but about seven, eight foot wide

Cats

or less. I'm leading him down there to get saddled, and I walk by that cat, that cat sitting up on that hay. And I have no earthly idea what possessed that dad-blamed cat to take a horseback ride. But that cat jumped down on the horse—right in the middle of that horse's back. And when it did, of course, that horse jumped. I'm assuming that that cat stuck all his claws in that horse's back. That horse, he run by me and knocked me down and he stepped on my knee when he went by me. I thought he broke my knee. But he went out of the barn, with that cat on his back, a-bucking! That horse was a-bucking, and I mean doing a good job of it, I might add!

My knee was hurt. I'm laying there in the barn and I'm looking out there at that horse, a-bucking with that cat on him and that cat's riding him, and he bucks out there in front of my barn. And I'm thinking all the time, *Oh, my gosh, he's going to buck right down there to that four-lane highway. I don't know how big of a wreck and how many people they're gonna kill,* and all that. I'm laying there, and I can't do nothing about none of it. That horse, he bucked out there in front of that barn, and made a big ol' circle. And here directly, he run under one of them mesquite tree limbs, and he knocked that cat off.

When he knocked that cat off, he quit bucking. But that horse was scared plumb to death. He come running back toward that barn, coming inside that barn, running wide open, trying to go back to his stall. When I seen him coming, I had to roll underneath the stall gate or that horse was gonna run back over the top of me. He went down there to his stall, and his eyes was about to pop out of his head. He got in that stall and he stood there, blowing like a rhinoceros.

I finally got up. I don't know where the cat went. But I hobble down there and close the stall gate, It took me probably a good thirty minutes or so to half-walk, half-crawl back to the house. My knee was hurt bad, and my britches leg torn. I go in the house, I take my britches off and I'm looking at my knee—it's all skint. I got me some ice out of the freezer and I got me an old towel. I go over there and turn the TV on. I'm laying on the couch, I got that ice round my knee, and about ten minutes later, ol' Dee comes home from work. It was very unusual, when she comes in the house, to see me laying on the couch. Immediately, she said, "Oh, my Lord, how bad are you hurt?"

I said, "Well, I don't know exactly for sure." I told her what happened, but when I'm telling her this story, she gets tickled, and she goes to laughing.

She said, "You mean that cat was riding that horse and never did come off of him? A-bucking? He's riding that bucking horse?" I said yeah. And she got tickled ... she thought that was dad-blamed funny.

It didn't break nothing in my knee. But there wasn't no horseshoeing and there wasn't no horseback riding. There was laying around the house for about ten days because that knee had swelled up so, and I couldn't hardly get around. But it finally got all right and so I got back to doing all that other stuff.

Then later on, a few months later, them two old cats were still hanging around there. I had a club-cab pickup at that time, and in the summertime, I parked it in the garage and left the windows down. I got out there one morning, started that truck up—I'm moving around there—I go to the barn and feed the horses. I take off and I'm headed north to Abilene, going about sixty miles an hour down the highway. That stupid cat. I guess he was laying under the pickup seat. I don't know for sure where the thing was in the back of that club-cab. All at once, he jumped up there by my shoulder and then jumped and hit me right in the chest. Scared me plumb to death and it's a wonder that I hadn't had a wreck! He jumped out the window with me going sixty miles an hour. When I looked in the rearview mirror, I seen cat and cat hair flying. That cat is rolling all over the pavement and all that hair flying off him and I just kept a driving. I went on and shod my horses, but that cat scared me plumb to death. That cat, he never showed back up, and I think we could just write that cat off.

A few months later, I'm going out to my buddy's house. I'm hooked onto my gooseneck. I've got my horse loaded. We're gonna shoe horses all day and we're gonna rope that evening. I'm driving down the highway, and I get about three miles from the house. I'm going about sixty miles an hour down that highway, and I just happened to look in my rearview mirror. That other yellow cat has jumped out of my gooseneck trailer with me going down the highway. Once again, it hit out there in the bar ditch, and it rolled. Fur went everywhere. And I thought, well, that cat's gone too. I didn't even stop. I went on out there to my buddy's house, and when I got out there, I went back there to unload my horse. I heard this *meow, meow, meow, meow.* That cat had done had three kittens up there in the gooseneck part of my trailer—three little ol' baby kittens. And I thought, *Lord have mercy ... what am I going to do with these dad-blame little babies?* But they're just sweet and fluffy, you know, and I said to myself, "I don't know what I'm going to do with them. I don't want to have to raise them things, with a bottle and all that."

My buddy had come out there by that time, and he said, "What are you doing?" I said, "I've got some addition to my cat population here." And told him what had happened and all that. He said, "Hey, I got a mama cat, and she just had a litter of kittens two days ago." He said, "Let's get them three cats and we'll just lay them there and see if she'll take them." We did, and they went to sucking that mama, and sure enough, that old cat, she raised them kittens just like they were hers—never had no problems.

I was out there about maybe six months after that roping at the house. And I just happened to look up and coming across my driveway was that one yellow cat that had them kittens in the trailer! And that old cat, I think it had done something to its brain because it wasn't walking too straight. It was kind of walking sideways and not very good at all. But it came into the barn, and I fed it and all. It hung around there, oh I don't know, probably three or four months after that. I was saddling horses up and leading them down to the other end of the arena. I had lights for my arena on telephone poles, and I looked up there. At the top of this dad-blamed telephone pole was that yellow cat. She was sitting right on top of that telephone pole. What she was doing up there, I have no earthly idea.

But I could remember. That cat's buddy had jumped down on that horse a long time ago. When I led a horse by, I was way out away from that telephone pole. I didn't want that cat to jump down on another horse and cause another wreck like that. When I got almost down to the other end of the arena, all of the sudden, instead of that cat crawling down that pole—the pole that was thirty foot high—he just bailed off, hit the ground, rolled back twice, got up, and just kind of staggered off. It didn't bother that cat a bit in the world. He hung around there for several years until we moved, and I don't know what happened to it after that.

Them dad-blamed cats, they cause problems sometimes around them horses, and you need to beware. They get underneath the horse, or you get to walking around, leading the horse or doing something, and they get right under your feet. They'll dang sure cause you a little bit of trouble.

When was in the army, I was sitting down there at an old boy's place where we'd been roping. We sat up there in the backyard, going to eat hamburgers and drank some homemade wine. This boy's daddy, he had about seven or eight little half-grown kittens. And we're sitting there drinking on that homemade wine, cooking hamburgers, and having the biggest time you ever did see, talking about roping and all this. Them cats were just laying around everywhere and I'm looking at them. That old boy's daddy, he said, "I bet you a dollar you can't catch one of them cats."

They're just laying everywhere, and I said, "Yeah, I can catch one of them cats. I'll just bet you that dollar." We're drinking on that wine, and here in a minute, one of them cats came over and laid down pretty close to me. He turned around and went to licking his back foot. When he did, I just reached down there, and I grabbed him, and I caught him right behind the shoulders. When I caught that cat, that cat went, *Arrrrrrgh,* and had all his claws sticking out in the air. I mean, he was mad, but he couldn't do nothing to me the way that I was holding him round the middle. That old boy's daddy, he went to laughing because I had him there. Didn't really know what I was going to do with the cat, other than throw him down. He said, "I lost my dollar, but I'll bet you another dollar you can't scratch him on the back of the neck."

I said, "Why, yeah, I can scratch him on the back of the neck!" I held that cat in my arm, and I run my other hand down my arm. I reached up there to scratch him with my finger between the ears. But I didn't really realize that a cat can almost turn his head plumb around on his body in a circle. That cat, he reached around there, and he bit me through the finger. And I mean, the blood flew. I throwed that cat down, and oh, boy, he got tickled! He laughed. Blood was flying everywhere, bleeding out of my finger. My buddy went in the house, got me some Campho-Phenique and washed it all up. We all had a pretty good laugh. But I don't really like cats.

26

TEETH

I TOOK some team roping horses out to California and made the deal with an old boy to stay at his place. The plan is I'm gonna sell these Texas team roping horses in California—they're gonna bring more money. And my ol' daddy, he's going to go with me. We had seven head of horses that we're going to take out there. Well, my daddy, he had just cut the tip end of his finger off roping. Got it in his dally, and he had that thing all bandaged up. He decided that he'd just ride with me out there. He couldn't do nothing else at the house anyway, since he had a big old bandage on that finger.

We load them horses up, and we take off to California with them. I'm driving. We're going across New Mexico ... going across Arizona. I'm going across Arizona at nighttime because I didn't want that heat to blow out tires. It's late at night, probably around three o'clock in the morning. I'm driving along and you can't see very good in the cab of one of them trucks—we just had a single cab truck. My daddy's sitting over there, and he's got his head over there against that window and he's asleep.

My daddy had false teeth. His top teeth got pulled out years ago, and he had a top plate that he got. He was too tight to let the dentist make him a top plate that fit right. One of his farming buddies said, "I got a brother who's got a funeral home. You can go down there to that funeral home, and he's got a whole bucket full of false teeth. You can just pick you some out." He goes down there and sure enough, he comes back home with a top plate of false teeth. And of course, they didn't fit very good. He was always taking them out and scraping them with his knife —they'd have a rough place on them that was making his gums raw. He was always scraping on them things.

When we were coming into California, we had to stop and let them look at the papers on them horses. They had a guard light. I thought he was plumb asleep over there— he hadn't moved or nothing. We come to that first guard light and out of the corner of my eye, my daddy has got his head over against that window, he ain't snoring or nothing, but he's got his mouth about half open and that top plate was just about half-falling out of his mouth. And my gosh, he looked like a skeleton. It scared me to death—I thought he was dead. I hit him on the shoulder. I said to wake up. He hit his hurt finger and he said, "What's the matter with you?" That scared me to death. I said, "Just wake up. You look like a dang dead skeleton over there!"

We get on out there to California and we get them

horses put up. We had leased some steers right down the road from this feller's house. And that old boy, we decided that we were gonna give him part of the profits on them horses for letting us come out there, him advertising these Texas horses, and using his place and all that. He had made arrangements for these steers, and we got ten steers down the road there. We also brung in four or five little wild burros off a desert. We were gonna rope them too.

The next day, we run them steers through and we had about six guys coming over there to try these horses. They come over there and Daddy is working the chutes. That's all he can do is load the steers and work the chutes. I'm roping on a heading horse, and I'd done sold a couple of heel horses. And these other four guys over there, they're talking and looking at a head horse, and one of them is trying another heel horse. We're roping and they're trying, and they're asking questions, and I'm really busy trying to sell horses and all that.

They'd been feeding these old steers some culled carrots. These steers were fat and slick, their hair looked pretty and stuff, but when they would go to the bathroom, it was pretty thin. It was same color as carrots. We're roping and roping and a-roping. I don't know how many steers we rope. My daddy's loading them steers, and he's just turning them out for us. I know we done run probably thirty head of steers on these horses, and this one old boy, he's going to buy this heel horse. Said he's gonna rope two or three more. There was one steer left in the chute, and he's in the chute ready to get roped.

Teeth

We're riding back to the chute and this guy's asking me a question about that heel horse.

My daddy is on his hands and knees behind that steer. He is on the outside of the chute, in the box, but he's on his hands and knees. He's got him a stick and he's digging around where them steers had been pooping while standing in that chute. Of course, I'm trying to tend to business and rope this man another steer. I finally ride up there and said, "What are you doing?"

He said, "I'm going to tell you something. You guys have been roping, just having a big time, with all that swapping horses, and buying horses, and talking about horses, and I ain't done nothing but work—load these steers and turn them out for you." And he said, "I got to coughing a while ago for some reason and I coughed my false teeth out. They're down here in this steer poop somewhere." About that time, he found them with that stick, and he said, "Oh! Here they are!"

Them other three boys, they're standing over there, and they're laughing. Two of them are sitting on horses, and they just about fall off their horses from laughing. And Daddy, he gets off his knees and goes over at the water trough, and he washes them false teeth off. He rubs on them and washes them off. Directly, he gets them clean as he can possibly get them, and he sticks them back in his old mouth and said, "That tastes just like carrot juice!" And that did tear all of them cowboys up. Oh ... they laughed and got tickled at that!

We sold some horses and then had another boy come

to look—he was an ex calf-roper. He had hurt his knee and wanted to start team roping, so he was gonna buy him a heeling horse. But he didn't heel very good. These little wild burros, you could rope them things—head and heel them—since they're wild little old things. I roped him a little old burro and he tried to heel him. The man missed that burro—he missed three or four times. I'm trying to tell him what he's doing wrong, and he finally gets frustrated. He just gets off that horse and said, "I'll just go down there and I'll flank that little burro. Take your rope off."

I said, "Well, you can do that if you want to, but I don't think it'd be a good id-dea." He didn't pay no attention to that. He jumped off that horse, he put his arm over that rope, and he run down there at that little old burro on the end of that rope. And that rope is coming out right beside that burro's mouth. When his hand got to that burro's mouth, that burro reached and grabbed the man's hand with his mouth. Burro bit him, and had a hold of him, and then clamped down on it like a bulldog. Wouldn't turn him loose! And that roper, he's jumping around with that burro, and he's a-hollering and a-screaming. Finally, he took his other hand and hit the burro in the eye with his fist. Well, that turned him loose.

He said, "You just take him on down there to that stripping chute, and you can get your own stupid rope off!" That didn't work out too good for him—crushed his ol' hand—and his roping was over with for that day. But he did buy the horse!

27

ELECTRICITY AND HORSES ... NOT GOOD

I ROPED a lot of calves in my earlier days. Had three or four calf horses around there and roped a bunch off them. I'd done pretty good roping calves. My two best horses, when I'd get off of them, I'd have a jerk line on them, but that jerk line wasn't working very good. I'd get about halfway down that rope and I always wanted them horses to back up and kind of drag them calves to me. I'd get about halfway down that old rope, they'd stop, and I didn't like that too good.

An old boy told me about one of them bird dog collars —little shock collars. Put that on a horse and punch a button. A horse can't stand much electricity, but you don't really punch that button, just kind of glance at it and give them a little dab of shock. I got one rigged up on that breast collar on this one horse and went out there and roped the calf. My old daddy, he had that box with him. I get about halfway down that rope, I'm going to holler back at him, and he's going to hit that button, give him a little shot. Boy, this one horse—we done that to him, man, it worked like a charm! He jumped back, ya know, and gosh almighty, you could put that on that horse about once every six months, and it made him work like a charm every single time. So, we thought, that's a great idea!

This other horse, he got to doing the same thing, so we thought, that ain't no problem. We'd just stick that little shock collar right there on that little breast collar on him. It fixed that other horse—it worked great on him—bound to work good on this horse.

We get it all rigged up, and my old daddy's got that little box. I ride in there, and I go out there, and I rope me a calf. I get about halfway down that rope and I holler back, and my ol' daddy, he kind of glanced over that button, and give the horse a little juice. That horse, when that juice hit him, he pawed in the air, and he run just as straight down that rope toward me and that calf as he could go.

I've seen them football players get hit pretty hard by them so-called big linebackers, but I don't think none of them linebackers weighed 1200 pounds like that horse did, cause that horse hit me and knocked me down flat. I didn't have no air left in me—liked to killed me. Then he run off with my little old calf, run down there at the end of the arena dragging that calf. I got up and hobbled down there to the other end of the arena to see that horse just standing there. I thought my calf was dead, but I took rope off that calf and pumped a little air in him, and he got

Electricity and horses ... not good

up and staggered off. The calf's all right and I'm all right, so I get back on my horse and I ride back down there. My ol' daddy, he'd got another calf in that chute, and he said, "Maybe you rope another, and we'll try it again ... see how that works."

I didn't really think that was a good idea. I said, "I'm either going to have to quit roping calves on him or accept him just like he is." I didn't want no more of that electricity on that particular horse right there. That didn't work out very good!

28

SALE BARN HORSES

I WENT OUT TO CLOVIS, New Mexico, bought thirteen head of horses at that sale. Come back with them horses—gonna ride them, rope on them, see how they are, train on them, sell them, make money on them—all this and that. I get back home the next day, I saddle the horses up and go to riding and roping on them. There was about four really good horses out of them thirteen head. Rest of them, they'd buck you off, they'd do this, they'd do that—just a little bit of everything. This one horse, you could head steers on him, you could heel steers on him—a pretty good horse. But he didn't have no shoes on his feet.

I'd roped on him there for about a week, and thought I'd shoe him. I shod his front feet, no problem. I reached back there to run my hand down his back hip so I could shoe his back feet, thought it would be no big deal. When I run my hand down his hip, that dude fired with both back feet. I thought, *Hmmm ... I guess that's the hole in that horse.* There ain't no telling who he kicked or who he killed out there, whatever, or why he was at that sale. I imagine that's the reason he was at the sale. I didn't even shoe him. His feet was good enough anyhow ... didn't need no shoes on him back there.

I roped on him around there another week or two and had a little guy come by. He's trying to rope steers and he needed a horse. This ol' boy, he come out there and he's going to buy ol' Ben—that's the horse's name. I tell him all about him, I rope on him, he ropes steers on him, and he wants to buy Ben. Now, I'd had little ol' practice ropings, two times a week at the arena there, two nights a week. And I told him, I said, "Now, I'm going to show you something about this horse. He ain't got no shoes on his back feet, and he don't need no shoes on his back feet. And this is the reason why." I put my hand on that horse's hip bone, run my hand down his hip and got about halfway down there, and sure enough, he fired both back feet. And I told that boy, said, "You see that?" He said, "Yes, sir, I see it." And I said, "You just leave his back end alone. I don't even want you to brush him back there." He said, "I can handle that. That's good for me."

This guy was learning to rope. He made his living as a meter reader, and he actually wore out one of them steer head dummies roping it. He'd put that dummy in the back of his pickup. He'd go around reading them meters. At lunch, he'd eat him a sandwich and he'd spend the rest of his hour roping that dummy. Anyway, he buys that horse, and I said, "I ain't gonna sell you that horse right now. Leave him here, and you come rope on him three or four more times, to make sure y'all are gonna get along real good." He said, "Okay, that's fine."

So, he winds up and he buys the horse, and he takes him home. He had a gooseneck cow trailer, and he took him home in that big gooseneck cow trailer. The next day he's gonna come back to rope, practice, on him at the house. He pulls up there in a two-horse, side-by-side trailer—a nice little ol' two-horse trailer. We're already roping out there and he pulls in the driveway. He turns around there, and I noticed he's got some ropes on the back—there ain't no tailgate on that trailer. He's got one of his ropes crisscrossed across there. I ride over there and said, "What in the world's the deal with these ropes right here?"

He said, "Well, I loaded ol' Ben in that trailer. When I closed that trailer door, gosh almighty, he went to kicking with both back feet, and he kicked the door plumb off that trailer—ruined it! This is my sister's trailer. I don't know what I'm going to tell her." I said, "Well, you're going to tell her that he's kicked the door off, and you're going to ask her how much it's gonna cost to fix it, because you're going to have to pay for it."

He comes back the next week with his cow trailer. He's riding around the arena. We're already roping, and when he come out in the arena, the whole side of his face, it looked like you peeled it about half the size of my hand

Sale barn horses

off his cheekbone. He ain't got no hide on there—it's blood-raw red. He didn't say nothing, so I finally asked him. It got the best of me I had to know. I figured ol' Ben done kicked him or done something to him. So, I finally asked him—I said, "Feller, what in the world has happened to the side of your face?" He said, "Oh, I was on my four-wheeler going to pen some cows and I hit a trail. That four-wheeler flipped and skint my face all up." I said, "Oh, well, good ... I'm glad it wasn't ol' Ben." He said, "Oh no! Ben is just fine!"

But we're roping—me and my buddy—we show up at a roping 'bout a month or two later. That guy, he's been roping on ol' Ben—he's roping real good—he's won some money and stuff. Everybody is outside the arena, pulled up to the arena, and me and my buddy, we pull in there and we pass by that ol' boy, and he's saddling ol' Ben up. And he waves at us—we wave and we go down there and park, we unload our horses, and our horses are done saddled. We're walking back towards the secretary's office to pay our entry fees. We're about two trailers down from where ol' Ben is—we can't see him—he's in between two trailers. And we get right down there at that trailer, and all at once, that ol' boy, he comes flying out of there and he makes two flips and lands out there on the ground right in front of us. And I said, "Holy mackerel!! What in the world happened?"

He said, "Oh, Bob," while holding his hip, said, "it's ol' Ben. I fooled around there and was gonna brush his rear end off. I forgot about what you told me. Oh man, he kicked me out here and I won't never forget it no more!"

I said, "Well, it's a good thing!" and we helped him up. But he kept that horse till he died, and I guarantee you that horse never got brushed on his rear end ever again! Wonder that it hadn't killed him!

29

DANCIN' GIRLS

So, I go to the big Lazy E Arena, a big steer-tripping up there in Guthrie, Oklahoma. Two ol' boys went with me, two of my steer-tripping buddies. We get up there the night before, put our horses up at the arena, and come back to town to get a motel. This one guy—he's got more money than me and this other ol' boy—he's going to stay at a nice motel. Me and this other guy, we're gonna stay at an ol' Motel 6 on down the street. The ol' boy said, "You all can stay down there at that Motel 6, but they got a real good bar in this thing." Said we can come in there and have some drinks—have a big time—visit with all the other ropers and all that stuff. We agreed, let's do that.

We walk up there at that nice bar—big ol' doors there—and we open them doors and walk in. There ain't even hardly dancing much yet, it's still pretty early. And this one old boy, he saw one of our buddies and he's telling an old roping story. I look across that dance floor, a pretty good ways across that little old dance floor, and there's three of the best-looking women I've ever laid my eyes on. They're sitting up there at a big old tall, round table up there. They got them a couple of drinks there and are smoking cigarettes. I tell my buddy there—he loved to dance just like I did—I said, "Look over there. Look at them three gals over there." He looked. He said, "Yeah ... go over there and see if they'll dance with you."

I walk over there, and I mean, they look real, so I walk up there and of course, that bar's kinda dark. I get up there to them and it's just three dummies. I laughed and turned around, start back across that dance floor, and he meets me halfway across. He said, "What's wrong—them girls wouldn't dance with you? Surely one of them would dance with you." I said, "No. That's just three old dummies!" He said, "We don't care how smart they are—let's go over and dance with them!"

I said, "Well ... go over and see if they'll dance with you." He walked over there and he sees that there's just three mannequins sitting there. He said, "By George, Lordy mercy, they are dummies, ain't they?"

We all had a laugh, and we go over and we sat with them—all three of us guys do. We got them girls sitting in our laps, and we're hugging on them and loving on them and all that. Our buddies are coming into the bar, and we're waving at them, and they're pretty jealous about our dummies. I've got one mannequin up and I'm a-dancing with her. They had a good band in there and they're

Dancin' girls

playing some good Western music. I danced with that mannequin, having a big time with her.

At the end of the bar, I don't know what was the matter with this feller. He ain't bothering nobody, but he'd been sitting at that bar. I guarantee he'd been in there an hour, had him a little old drink, and had his head down. I don't know what kind of problems that feller had, but he just ain't bothering nobody—he's just sitting there and having a little old drink and just looking down at the bar the whole time ... ain't bothering a soul.

They played one of them old Western swing songs—a pretty good fast song. And man, I'm dancing with my mannequin dummy! I sling her around and one of her legs comes off—comes flying off. It hit that slick dance floor and it slid about thirty foot across that dance floor — and landed right under that fellow's bar stool! It scared him to death. He jumped up there and he run plumb out of that bar—he left!

I go over and I get her leg, bring her back over to the table, and we plop her up on that little old round table there. Me and my buddies, we went to trying to poke that leg back in there and get it put back on. And I don't know how them legs go on them mannequins. We couldn't figure it out.

We never did get that leg on. We had her laid up there and we was trying hard to get that leg on her—never did. So I just pick her up and I take her and her leg to that bartender and flop her up on that bar. I said, "Hey, let me give you my name, address and phone number, and you get this old baby doll fixed and send me the bill. I'll be glad to pay for it since I tore her up!"

He said, "Oh, just don't worry about it. As much fun as we've had out of you three idiots over there with them three dummies in this bar tonight—just don't worry about it. We'll just get her fixed up. Pay her no mind." So we went to the steer roping and had a big time and all that.

30

HAVIN' FUN CAN GET SERIOUS

Later on, through the years, my son, he got in the movie business. There was an old actor—good ol' boy—ol' cowboy actor. He had about four different charity rodeos, where they team roped, cut, team pen, all that kind of stuff. He had sports celebrities and singing stars and movie stars and all that come there. They were raising money for children's cancer and research and all that. It was a great deal, raised a lot of money, for several years. We got to going to them things.

We went to one of them deals, at the little bar and little party that night—everybody's having a big time. The word leaked out that it just so happened to be my birthday. Two of my good friends—cowboy friends—long about 12 o'clock, they stopped the party and made a big announcement. Stopped the band, told everybody that it's Bob's birthday—we're gonna celebrate Bob's birthday. They looked all over town trying to buy me a present.

They went to one of them, some kind of place, where they had these blow-up dolls—these naked blow-up dolls. They presented me with this blow-up doll in the bar. They thought they was gonna embarrass me. Well ... I just danced with her all night, the rest of the night—had a big time and all that and had a lot of fun! When I got back home, I just put that old blow-up doll in the top of the closet. Forgot all about her.

Like I've said, I lived on a major four lane highway. Right down the road there—just about an eighth of a mile from my house—there's a major intersection there. I'd been riding a horse, training on him. It was hot, a little bit before dark, and I had that horse real hot. I thought, well, I'll just kinda ride him around, down in the bar ditch, and let him cool off a little bit. It was just at dusk, and I didn't have no idea what made me stop and think about that blow-up doll in that closet. But I thought it'd be funny if I got that doll down. I tied a red wild rag around her neck. I brought her out there, got on that horse and I stabbed her down on the saddle behind me.

I'm riding down the bar ditch and it's a busy highway. I mean, there's people slowing down, there's people honking, there's people waving. They think I got a naked girl on behind me on that horse. I'm having a lot of fun doing that, while I'm riding down toward this intersection. When I get down there to that intersection, I turn and I head west. There's an old boy—he's coming and he's looking at my little doll on the back of that horse. All at once, he realizes that he needs to stop at the stop sign, and

Havin' fun can get serious

he stomps them brakes. And let me tell you, he slides them brakes all the way through that four-lane intersection. How there was not a car coming, I don't know!

It scared me to death. All I can think about is if there'd been a car coming, they'd have hit each other, there'd have been people killed, and would be the biggest wreck. It scared me to death, something like that happening. Let me tell you what ... I pulled my pocket knife out and I stabbed that baby doll in the leg—let all the air out of her. I loped that horse back to the house and throwed that old thing in the trash. All I was trying to do, just have a little fun ... but sometimes fun cannot turn out so good!

31

MAD WOMEN

ME AND OL' Daddy, we hook our two-horse inline trailer and we head off to East Texas, to meet up with our other team roping partner. We're going to one of our CRA —Central Rodeo Association—rodeos to team rope. We get down there, but we blowed out a tire going down there. We're running a little late to the rodeo. It had rained a bunch, and it's muddy all around that rodeo. We're trying to find a place to park—can't find a place to park— and we need to get there and get on our horses because we're fixing to get our steer turned out. We just pull up to a spot and we stop, get out, unload them horses, and saddle them right quick. They're just about calling our name out to rope when we meet up with our other buddy. We rope our steers and we done real good. It's Saturday night, and we placed in the rodeo, so we got money.

Me and my ol' daddy, we go back out there and people's leaving the rodeo. This arena is right in a residential section—right in the middle of town—so we're trying to figure out how in the world we were going to get out. Figured we were stuck. Our buddy, he comes out there and we tell him that we've gotta figure out how to get out. Said we think we're stuck … may have to get pulled out. I didn't know, but that being said, I tell him, "You go up there and get our money after the bull riding is over with. Get our money, pick it up, and then we'll leave."

We go to trying to figure out how we're going to get out. We still got the horses saddled and there's a bunch of houses there. We looked down aways, and there was what looked like kind of an alley down there with a guard light down there. We could see pretty good. We figured we'd ride down there, since we couldn't back up too good with that inline trailer in that mud. We figured that I'd drive down there, fool around there, and see if we can come out on the street down there. It looked like a pretty decent little alleyway there.

I fooled around there, and my daddy, he's riding a horse and got a flashlight. I get in the truck. He's leading another horse with his other horse, and he motions for me to come on with that light. And here I go—I gas that truck and here I come. I'm slinging mud, man, I'm slinging mud all down that alley. Daddy hollered at me that there's a bar ditch and told me to stomp on it. So, I stomp on it pretty good and come right out there—under that guard light—out there on the pavement. There's houses right there, and we don't think nothing of it—we pull out there on that pavement.

My daddy gets off that horse, and about that time, a back porch light comes on, and there is a woman that come out to her back porch—and she is a very large woman! She's going to tip them scales pretty good along 285 pounds or so! She's big and she has got the dad-blamedest get up on—she's got this house coat on. She's got these big, humongous curlers in her hair—all rolled up in her hair—and she looked like some kinda Martian. And she's got on big, fuzzy Pink Panther house shoes. She comes out and she is mad—not a little mad—I mean, she is mad! Stomping out there, raising cane, and she's a-cussing. She said, "You idiot cowboy! You run through my backyard, and you done rut it all up!"

And I'm there unsaddling horses and my daddy is talking to her—well, trying to talk to her. She's just berserk ... she is going crazy. He's trying to calm her, and she says, "I can't believe two idiots just run through somebody's backyard, got it all rutted up." She said, "It's going to cost money to fill all these ruts in ... that's just stupid! I can't believe y'all done something like that!" And my daddy is saying, "Yes ma'am, you're sure right. We did not know that. We're trying to apologize." Then he said, "I'll tell you what, you take my business card and you hire somebody tomorrow, when it dries up, to fix your ruts and send me the bill and I'll be glad to pay for it."

I'm unsaddling horses over there and she is just out of her head—she is absolutely crazy. She ain't taking his business card—she's just stomping around there and cussing us, saying that she can't believe what we had done. By the time I got one horse unsaddled—that woman—she's standing in front of my daddy, and she takes her right hand and she comes around and she slaps my daddy upside the head. And when she did, she turned right on around, had her back to him, and she's going to go back to the house. My daddy, he ain't never hit a woman before in his life, but when she slapped him like that, it just got all over him. It was just a reaction—he kicked her in the rear with his boot, and he stabbed that big old house coat right up the middle of her butt. She squalled like a wild Comanche and she took off to that house. She's calling the law—her brother-in-law—the sheriff. My daddy, he turns around to me, and he says, "Robert, I think it's time to go!"

We throw them horses in that trailer. We get in that truck, and we're driving off. We got to go back there and find our buddy. He's probably wondering what in the world has happened to us. My daddy gets out of the truck, and he slips back through them other houses and stuff. He goes back there and finds our team roping buddy—he's got the truck all started and warmed up—and Daddy gets in with him.

We're gonna meet up. I start out driving, and we're gonna meet about sixty miles down the highway at the all-night truck stop. We're gonna meet up there. Daddy gets in his truck, and he tells our buddy, he said, "When you get in this truck, you drive right! Don't you speed. You stop at every stop sign, and you use them directional lights, whatever. You do not break the law!" Our buddy, he's wondering what the world's going on. We ain't told him anything yet. But as I pull away, and I get about a quarter of a mile from that gal's house, here come three squad cars up there with lights and sirens going. They pull up there in front of her house and I guess that crazy woman—we've got an inline trailer—I guess she never looked at that trailer to describe what in the world kinda rig that we're driving in.

I got on out of town. My daddy and team roping partner, they get out of town—drove that sixty miles out to that all night truck stop. I'm in there sitting down at the table. The waitress, she done brought me a cup of coffee. Whenever they get there, they walk in, and let me tell you what, that woman hit my daddy pretty good, because when he walked in and sat down at that table, you could still see four red finger marks on the side of his cheek. But I don't know why that lady was upset and still wish she'd just settled down and figured out it was an accident. We didn't mean to do that, and we'd have been glad to pay for it, but never did hear nothing either which way. We never did go back to that rodeo, though, and when it'd come back around once a year, we'd never go back to that town. We didn't think it was a good idea-y!

32

MACHINE GUNS

ONE DAY the army come got about a dozen of us MPs, and we're gonna go do some training. We got these Jeeps—these two Jeeps—and they got these fifty-caliber machine guns mounted on the back of them Jeeps. They've got a firing range there, and it's ten-foot high, like a big tank dam. But you drive up on it and then you drive down the other end of it. The deal was, you pair up—one of you drives—they want you to drive pretty good speed on top of that tank dam. They got targets out there, and one of you drives while another one shoots the machine gun. You're shooting at them targets to see if you can hit them. When you get down at the other end, you're going to turn around, and you're going to swap spots.

The boy I was partnered up with, I didn't know him, but I start out driving. I get in that Jeep; he's standing in the back. I drive up one side, drive along there, and he's shooting that machine gun. I don't know whether he's hitting anything or whether he ain't. I'm busy a-driving. I come off the other end of the dam—roll off it—I turn that Jeep around, and we swap. He gets in there and drives—it's my turn to shoot. He comes back up on that tank dam; he's driving along and I'm a-shooting. I'm hitting them targets pretty good. We get about halfway down that little firing range and all at once he runs that Jeep off the side of that tank dam, off the side of that big old mound of dirt. Holy mackerel—thank goodness he's driving fast enough. It turned that Jeep over and it threw us plumb out of that Jeep. Thank the Lord, it threw us away from that Jeep to where it wouldn't roll over on top of us! It skinned us up pretty good—tore that gun, that machine gun—up, bent the barrel on it and all that. Holy mackerel!

I look up, and here comes a Jeep down through there, with a captain, a major and a sergeant in that Jeep, and they come down there. Of course, I thought they'd get out of that Jeep to see if we was all right. Well, they didn't care whether we was all right, or whether we wasn't all right. They was mad and cussing us, 'cuz we'd done tore their little gun up and they didn't care whether we was hurt, whether we wasn't hurt.

I asked that old boy, "What in the world caused you to drive off that mound of dirt?" He said, "I got to watching what you were shooting at there—to see if you was hitting them targets. I didn't realize it, but that's how come I drove off of it." I said, "If we wind up having to do this,

Machine guns

then there in Nam, I'm going to find me a different partner than you." He said, "I don't blame you a bit in the world!" We lucked out. I guess, once again, the good Lord looked out after me because all it did was just skint us a little bit.

33

BAD SHOT

I HAD a good friend of mine—just like a brother to me. He bought cattle, roped, was a good cowboy and all that. They had a sale barn and a bunch of pens behind his house. They lived right there by the sale barn. He was always buying little old sick calves and stuff to fool around there. He had four or five in a pack of dogs that come around at night—he lived right there close to town—and these town dogs come out there. They had killed two or three of them little old sick calves and he was teed off about that. He was always trying to get the dog catchers to come out there and catch them dogs. He told them what's going on and all that. The dog catcher, he never would come out there—wouldn't nobody do nothing about it.

He decided he's going to shoot them dogs. He always had a nice truck, nice trailer, all that—good equipment—because he used them every day, every single day. He would pull up sometimes—he'd come in from them sales

Bad shot

late at night—he'd just pull up there at the yard gate, step out tired and just give out. And he'd just go in the house and go to bed. He decides that he's gonna try to shoot two or three of them dogs. They wouldn't come out except at nighttime. One of them calves had died. He got that calf and he drug him up there in the yard, right there by the door—by the back door. He had pulled in the yard—that truck and trailer—he had it parked up there long ways.

He got his shotgun, put his shotgun right by the door, and went to bed. Sometime during the night, he heard them dogs out there eating on that calf, growling around there and trying to fight one another. He crawls out of that bed, and I don't know why he did this—but this is what his wife tells me—he is in his drawers and he slips his boots on. I don't know why he puts his hat on, but he puts his hat on. She said that was funny enough, but he grabs that shotgun, puts his hand on that doorknob, and I mean, he flings that door open and steps out on that porch and ... BOOM. Boom, boom, boom, boom! Had the plug out of that gun, so he had five shells in that shotgun.

He heard one of them dogs yelp. He comes back in, closes the door, and sets the gun down. Comes back to bed. He's proud of himself, he knows he's done shot two or three of them dogs. The next morning—come daylight—his wife's in the bathroom getting ready to go to work. He's getting dressed, tells her bye, and he steps outside that door and his wife hears the dad-blamedest cussing. Of course, this boy was a good job—he'd done a good job at that cussing anyway—but he's a-cussing and a-raising cane out there and is madder than an ol' wet hen!

She runs out there and said, "What in the world's the matter?" He said, "Just look ... just look!" I mean, there ain't a dead dog around—there ain't a dog around nowhere. But he has done killed two of them high-dollar Michelin trailer tires on his gooseneck trailer. He didn't hit a dog nowhere, but he'd done a good job on them tires. Killed them tires. Oh, he got mad. He finally got rid of the dogs, though.

34

COWS AND SOLDIERS

Down there in the army, like I've said, I had my horse down there with them boys and they run them cattle out there on that army reservation. There's about ten people that run cattle, had the lease on that army camp. Everything is open range out there—there ain't no pens—we gathered them cattle with dogs, them Catahoula cow dogs. There's a bunch of cattle up there, and lots of good roads through that army camp. So, we drive along and go out there might near every other day. The cows stayed in a certain area. I was with them one day and we were gonna go to the army camp and go out there. There was two or three calves we wanted to catch and take to sell, two or three more calves to work, and one old barren cow that ol' boy wanted to get rid of.

We're driving along on them roads. Got them dogs back of that truck, in the dog box. And as we're driving along there, we happened to see a bunch of these army boys. They're bivouacked—got their little army tents set up—they got about eight or ten of them army tents set up all in a good nice little straight line. Had their little guns and little tripods and all that. And there's a big old hill right there behind them. We drive by and they just kinda wave at us, we wave at them. We go on about a quarter of a mile and see some cows. We stopped, let them dogs out and those dogs get after them cows and boy, they bay them cows up. Them cows are used to them dogs around all the time. Them cows knew to just bunch up, and them dogs would circle them cows and hold them. You could ride in there and rope whatever you want. We roped a couple of them yearlings, load them in a trailer. Worked one baby calf.

But as you do that, them cows, they kinda move. And then them dogs would bay them up again and you roped another hot old Boran cow, and they'd move again. There was a couple more little calves we needed to work. So, we go to rope them cows, and they took off running and they come over that hill. We'd forgot all about them boys—that little bivouac area and them army boys. It was about lunchtime, and they was all sitting around under them trees, reading their mail. Them cows come over that hill in a little stampede and we was right after them. They run through there with them dogs right after them, barking and raising cane. Man, they come through that little bivouac area and they wrecked them guns and they run through them tents and scattered them guys—they was all hiding behind some cedar trees.

Cows and soldiers

It was a heck of a stampede right through their camp. And we went right on after them. A couple of them dogs bayed them up down there, and we stopped. Here come a captain and a couple of sergeants in a Jeep. And boy, they was mad! The last thing I seen, one of them cows—one of them big tiger-striped horned cows—she had one of them tents on her horns, going down through that brush. She is a-pawing at it and a-bellering at it. She tore their little tents all to pieces. We didn't mean to do that—we just forgot about them guys. But the ranchers, they had just as much rights or more to be out there working their cattle.

That captain, he come up there, we stop and he gets out a-cussing—cussing us cowboys. And I'm sitting on my horse—I ain't dressed army—I'm dressed like a cowboy, hat and all. That other boy, he was too. And that old boy's daddy, he was too. That captain, he's a-cussing us out—none too happy. After about three minutes of him chewing on us, that old boy's daddy, he let the captain quit cussing. He said, "Are you through?" And the captain said, "I guess."

That old daddy—he didn't take nothing off nobody—he jumped back at that captain. He said, "I'm going to tell you something. We got more rights here. We was out here before this army camp ever got here and were running cattle on this thing!" He kinda jumped back in the middle of the captain, and that was all over with. But it was pretty funny with all them cows stampeding down through there. That's just what happened out there on the army camp.

35

COWBOY ON THE BEACH

MY WIFE HAS GOT some good friends, and they had a girl who's gonna get married, and they're planning a big, huge wedding. They're gonna have it down there in Cancun, Mexico. We all gotta go—there's probably about fifty of us going to Cancun, Mexico—to celebrate at their wedding. They're gonna get married on the beach down there. I didn't really wanna go—didn't care nothing about Cancun. But of course, my wife wanted me to go, and they're good friends, so we all load up on a big old plane.

We get down there to Cancun, get our luggage, go to this nice, big, fancy hotel where all of us got reservations to stay. Then everybody runs down there to the old beach—they just couldn't wait to go down there to the beach. About seven or eight of the women in our little party, well, they didn't figure I had a bathing suit, so they bought me a present. They said, "We bought you a bathing suit." They had it in a little paper sack, and it was in their luggage.

Cowboy on the beach

I said, "That's fine and dandy. I probably won't get in the ocean anyway." The next day, everybody eats breakfast—they can't wait to go down there to that beach. Some of them were making plans for the wedding and all that—the wedding is gonna be the next day. We had all day just to mess around on that beach. They go to the ocean to swim, do what you do in the ocean and stuff, and they wanted me to get in there with them. They said, "We know you don't like the water, but go down there ... we're having fun. Go get your bathing suit on and come down there."

I said, "Well, all right." I go up there to the hotel room, asked Dee, and she said she had me a bathing suit packed. She's trying to tell me what suitcase it's in. I can't find it nowhere, but I see that paper sack and I said, "Them girls bought me one—it's in here." I dump it out on the bed and it's one of them—I didn't know what she called them then, but they told me later on—it's one of these Speedos, a little Speedo. And that Speedo is mighty tight. And there was a little old shirt there—a little t-shirt, little tight t-shirt. I'm looking at this little Speedo and wondering how in the world I'm going to get this little tight thing on.

I finally get that thing on—there ain't much to a little Speedo—I put that little tight shirt on. I get ready to come back down there to meet up with them. I put my boots on, put me some sunglasses on, put my cowboy hat on, and I come back down that elevator. I stepped off that elevator—it's in the evening by this time—and they had a

Mexican band there and there's people dancing now to that Mexican music.

I walked down through there and I'm a sight because I ain't really got a figure for a speedo. But I didn't really care—didn't make me no difference—I was just a-walking. The whole Mexican dance band stopped, and I just walked right on through them. All them people, they're dancing, so I tipped my hat to them and I said, "Qué pasa, amigos?"

I opened the doors, and down there between the motel and the beach, they had a humongous patio. There's four hundred people down there on that patio eating supper, drinking and having a big ol time. Let me told you what, whenever I opened them doors and stepped out there on that patio, you'd have thought Elvis walked out on there, because I ain't never seen so many flashbulbs go off in my life. My wife is already down there in the swimming pool part—they ain't even in the ocean—they're in the swimming pool part. And holy mackerel, she sees me standing up there, and I squall at her, I hollered for her! She's embarrassed and she just dives under the bar, to hide behind the bar.

I hollered out, "That ain't gonna do you no good! You brought me to this Cancun joint and you're stuck with me!" But it was a sight to see. I fooled around there and got in that little pool for a minute. Then we laid out there on that beach and I figured out pretty quick—when you get that beach sand in amongst that speedo, it ain't very comfortable. It'll gall you pretty quick! That was my little

Cancun wedding—we had the little wedding—and everybody had a good time. Got back home safe and sound. But I throwed that Speedo away—I didn't think I needed that no more!

36

A COWBOY AND HIS CITY PARDNER

FOR TWENTY-FIVE YEARS, in Abilene, I had a cow partner. His wife owned two places down there at Winters. Her old husband, he was a retired FBI man—he didn't know nothing about cattle. But his ol brother-in-law, his wife's brother, he run cattle down there and he got in bad shape and got in a nursing home. I'd have to go down there and help him pen some cows—did that a couple times—hauled them to the sale barn. That old boy, he's in too bad a shape to get out of the nursing home, so we made a deal to buy them cows and I leased the place. We partnered on them cows—had about eighty head of them things. And my old buddy, he couldn't do nothing without putting on a pair of gloves—and he smoked a pipe. I told him, I said, "You ain't gonna be a very good partner. Anybody that's gotta have gloves don't do anything. They're either looking for their gloves, or they're putting them on, or they're taking them off. And you

A cowboy and his city pardner

smoke a pipe, so you're either trying to light the pipe, or find your pipe tobacco, or smoking on it. Can't get no work out of you at all!" He said, "That's the way I do things!" We aggravated each other pretty bad, but all in fun.

I had pens right in the middle of this big old pasture. And that pasture was brushy, 1,200 acres of it. I had them cows trained to come to a siren. We'd fed them in them pens all the time. So, my cow partner, I always accused him of not having no rear end. I accused him of his wife chewing his rear end out many times that he didn't have no rear end left at all. He liked to go feed them cows. When I would feed them, I'd close all the gates, pour the cubes out, then go open the gates up to let the cows in. Well, he didn't like doing it that way. He wanted to feed them by just pouring out of a sack with them cows all around him. It's dangerous—I told him many times. I said, "Them cows are going to run over you. One of them is going to run over you and break your leg or something. You don't need to do it that way!" Well, he just had to do it that way—that's the way he done it.

We're down there one week, and I'm saddling my horse up to go check some water gaps. We blow that siren and here comes all them cows—there's about fifty of them coming in there. He gets his cake sack—he's got that pipe lit. He's not too far away from me, probably about fifty feet from me. He's pouring them cubes out and them cows are all around him. I just happened to look up and see his britches have fallen down around his ankles. He stumbles and falls down, pouring them cake sacks out. Them cows are all around him and all I can see is that pipe tobacco smoke—I mean, it looks like a chimney coming out of them cows. I holler, "What in the world? Crawl out of there and get out of them cows—they're gonna kill you!" He crawls out on his hands and knees, with his britches down there around his ankles, and gets over out of the way. And I don't know how, but ain't one dad-blamed cow even stepped on him! I guess the man upstairs was looking after him. I thought it was pretty funny looking though.

I got my stay wire, and went down there while he pulled his britches up, tightened his belt up one hole, and I made him a set of suspenders out of that stay wire, so that he could go ahead and feed them cows. And I went on off and checked my water gaps. But the next week when we went down there and I met up with him, he had a brand, spanking new set of red suspenders. That's what he wore the rest of the time. But wonder them stupid cows hadn't killed him.

37

RIDE THE RIGHT HORSE

My old daddy, he had an old doctor friend north of Dallas. We worked on his old horses—he had an old stud and about a dozen mares—he never done nothing with them horses. We'd break a couple colts every year, take them back down there, and just turn them loose. He didn't even want to ride them or nothing, but he wanted them broke. They never was messed with, except about every three months when he wanted us to come down there and trim their feet. He had an old barn there with a pretty good-sized lot. Some of them old horses, the only time they ever got caught, like I say, was once every three or four months when we'd go trim their feet. They was about like a bunch of broncs, and some of them wasn't even broke to fool around with. We'd take two horses down there and rope them things, head and heel them like steers, get them on the ground, and trim their feet that way.

Well, we gonna go down there one day in the springtime. In the wintertime, horses can get kinda thin—they wasn't very stout. But the springtime had good grass down there and they'd get fat and get pretty stout. We're going to go down there, and once again, my old daddy, he said, "I'll take this horse down here." We were riding this horse —breaking it for a fella. He said, "I can rope them mares, and you can heel them on your horse.

I said, "That horse ain't very big, Daddy, to rope them horses and stuff. We'll be yanking that horse you're riding around. He ain't too good a horse anyway." He said, "Oh yeah, he'll be all right."

We go down there, and that pen was like six boards high—a pretty high pen. We got there and we roped three or four of them things. I heeled them, while Daddy got off to trim. I'd hold them down, he'd trim their old feet, then he'd get back on this old horse—this one horse that he didn't have no business being on. He steps back on that horse and he roped a big old fat mare. She was running down the fence and she was coming to the corner. Right about the time she's gonna get to that corner, that's when the rope is gonna get tight. That all happened, and he had that mare roped a little bit too deep. She got to that corner and she didn't even slow up. She jumped that fence—and my daddy's tied on. She didn't get the fence cleared—she broke the top three boards off that fence. That little old horse my daddy was on, she drug that horse and my daddy through the other three boards. They went through there and I mean boards scattered and splintered every which way! She drug him about fifty foot out there in that pasture, before he finally got her stopped and turned around, got her back up there. The rest of them horses all run through that hole in the fence.

I said, "You want to turn her loose? You want to trim her feet?" And he said, "Might as well just heel her and go ahead and trim her feet." I don't know why it didn't hurt that little old horse he was riding, or stick a board in him or something other. We called that old boy up after we trimmed her and turned her loose and told him what happened. Said, "Reckon you can fix that fence—to get it all patched back up—and we'll come back and finish all the rest of them." That's what happened, but my daddy took a bigger, stouter horse down there that next time, and everything worked out a whole lot better.

38

SOMETIMES A CLOWN AIN'T FUNNY

WE'RE OUT THERE in West Texas, and we went to a lot of rodeos, a lot of ropings. There's a rodeo clown out there, that was a great rodeo clown, out there in that country. He worked a big part of them West Texas rodeos. He was funny. He was a bull-fighting rascal, and he had some clown acts—and I mean some good clown acts—that was just hilarious. Everywhere he went, he just enjoyed what he did out there in that arena. But there was a time or two that we'd get to that dad-gum rodeo and the law would show up. He'd done something on the way to that rodeo that wasn't quite right, so the law would come get him and take him off to jail. But they would always wait till after the bull riding was over with so he could clown them bulls. I don't know how he got out of trouble here, there, and yonder, but he did.

One particular rodeo was over July the Fourth. The clown told the stock producer and announcer, he said, "I

Sometimes a clown ain't funny

want to keep one extra roping calf in the chute, after the tie-down calf roping. I want to do something with that calf and fireworks" and said that it'd be funny. They told him that it was okay—that's fine. Now the calf roping is over with, and them calves—you run them through several times, and they know where the back end of the arena is—so, when you open the gate, you don't even need a horse. They're gonna kinda high lope down right through the center of the arena, and go down there back to the catch pen.

This clown, he takes one of them Roman candles and he gets in that shoot. He ties it on that calf's tail—ties it at the top and ties it at the bottom of that Roman candle. He said something to that announcer. That announcer, he's saying something about the rodeo clown—how he's his own way of celebrating July the Fourth. About that time, he lights that Roman candle and opens the gate and lets that calf out. Boy, it's dark, and that calf high lopes down the middle of that arena, and it's shooting them Roman candles up in the air—and boy, it's pretty. It's funny, and everybody's laughing and having a big time with it. That calf gets about halfway down that arena when one of them strings comes loose—whether it's the top one or the bottom—I don't know which—but it turned that Roman candle. And just as it did, that Roman candle shot one of the candles at the concession stand. It was halfway down the bleachers, halfway down that arena—and it fired one of them Roman candles right in that concession stand. It hit right in the corney-dog grease. And when that thing hit that grease, that grease splattered everywhere. And it set all that grease on fire.

The people in there—about three or four people in that concession stand—they all run out of there. It set that concession stand on fire! They didn't even come back in there to get the fire extinguisher and try to put it out. It burnt the concession stand plumb down because they didn't have no fire truck at the rodeo. They had an ambulance but didn't have no fire truck. It burnt that concession stand plumb down to the ground. They told that clown that that was a sure good act, but maybe we don't need to do that act next year for July the Fourth.

39

BE NICE TO YOUR LITTLE SISTER

My little sister, Cindy, was seven years younger than me. We'd fool around the ranch—we had about three acres there. The bull nettles would come up all around that place. Now, a bull nettle is a stinging nettle—they sting you. You'd touch them, and they'd sting ya! Well, they grew out there. My old daddy, he's going to go work the fire station there one day. He had us a couple of wheelbarrows and a hoe, and he told me and my little sister, said, "Tomorrow, I want y'all to chop all them bull nettles, pile them up out there in that wheelbarrow so that in a day or two, when they're dry, we're going to burn them to get rid of them dad-blamed stinging nettles."

He left to go to the fire station, and me and her, we get out there. I'm a-looking and I was always trying to do something to my little sister, since she'd follow me around all the time, she'd be in my way anyhow. Now, I don't know the difference in these bull nettles –why some of them have a little yellow flower on them, and some of them have a little white flower on them. I can't remember which one had the most out there—the white ones or the yellow ones—but the ones that had the most of them, I told her, I said, "Those are heifer nettles. I'm going to chop the bull nettles, but you gotta chop the heifer nettles." I was out there probably two hours, and I got all my bull nettles chopped—all piled up—and she spent all the rest of the day out there in sun. She's chopping all them heifer nettles and I didn't help her because I told her I didn't have to. I'd done my bull nettles, she was to do the heifer nettles. She didn't know no difference—she just thought that's the way things was.

Well, I go off and do something else, and the rest of the day she's out there in that heat, doing all that. It was a terrible thing for me to do to her. My daddy, he comes home next day from the fire station. We're out there, and we meet up with him. Boy, he looked out there and said how good a job we'd did—had all them stinging nettles all piled up in some piles—and he's bragging on us. Told us how good a job we've done. My little sister, she said, "Daddy, it took me all day. Bob got through pretty quick with his bull nettles, but there was a whole lot more of them heifer nettles that I had to chop, but I got it all done! It took all the rest of the day."

He said, "What do you mean ... heifer nettles?" And she told him what I had told her, and he said, "Excuse me just a minute." He went to his pickup—he had a pair of old welding gloves on—them gloves got a sleeve on them that comes all the way up your arm to your elbow. He put them two welding gloves on, and he walked out there. He got me and Cindy, and we walked out there in the middle of all them stinging nettles and he said, "Bull nettles and heifer nettles, huh?"

He grabbed me by the arm, and he picked up one of them big bull nettles, and he commenced to whooping me over the back, over the butt, and over the head with that stinging nettle—everywhere. He whooped me till there was nothing left of that bull nettle to even hit nothing with. He said, "I can't believe you done that to your little sister—made her work out there all day, and you just quit her!" But I deserved every bit of that. From then on, she knew the difference between bull and heifer nettles. But that was a mean thing to do—I should not have done that to my little sister, but I did, and I got punished for it.

40

COWBOY FISHIN'

My wife, her kinfolks—her brothers—they're all fishermen, hunters, and all that. We'd all get together, we'd come in from Abilene, for every holiday to visit and shoot the breeze, all that. For years they'd been wanting me to go fishing with them, and I never cared nothing about it. But we came in one time and they all said something about it. They was planning a fishing trip the next day, going up to Lake Texoma—a big old lake. They said, "Come on, we want you to go with us. We're going to fish at night, so you ain't got no roping to go to—you can go." And I finally said, "All right, I'll go with you."

There was going to be two boats—two boatloads of us. We'd ate supper and loaded up to get out there. And we drive up there to that lake. It's not quite dark, but almost. We unload them two boats. We're on the Texas side of Lake Texoma, right between Texas and Oklahoma. We all get in the boats. I get in one boat with one of her

Cowboy fishin'

brothers and one of her brothers-in-law. I'm sitting in the back of the boat, and we go across the lake—they drive that boat across the lake. Other boat goes also—two of her brothers also go across there. We all go across that lake in them boats. It's dark time. We get across that lake, pull up to this pier, and go out into the lake. We pull up there at that pier and tie them boats up. They said, "All right, let's get out and unload our fishing stuff. We're going to fish off this pier."

And I thought it's kind of strange because there was cars on that side of the lake. I wondered, so I asked them, I said, "Couldn't we have just drove around here on this side of the lake and drove right up to this pier?" They said, "Yeah, we could have, but we didn't need to. You gotta fish in the boat—gotta come across here in the boat." I don't know nothing about fishing, so that's just fine and dandy.

Anyhow, we fish—and I didn't realize—I just thought we were going to fish a few hours and go home, but we fish all night long. All night! And we catch fish—I catch four or five—and they caught a whole mess of them, these croppies or crappies, whatever, crappy cop—whatever they call them fishes. But that's what we was catching, catch a mess of them. It's beginning to kinda crack daylight.

All at once, they said, "Well, it's getting daylight—let's go." We go, load everything up in the boat, and here we go. Sun's about to get where you can see, and I'm tired, I'm ready to go home. I'm sitting in the back of the boat. Her old brother and her brother-in-law, they're up there driving the boat and they're talking. I'm sitting there in the back, and we're going across the lake. It. I have to admit it was a beautiful, beautiful morning. The lake looked like a glass—there wasn't a breath of air—and that lake was still. It was absolutely gorgeous. The sun's coming up, and I'm looking at that sunrise and the clouds, and it's just absolutely beautiful. I'm sitting back there and I ain't really caring what they're doing, with that motor going, I can't even hear what they're saying. They're just talking to each other up there. One of them is pointing one way and one of them is pointing another way—one of them shakes his head and points another way—and I didn't realize it at the time, but they was looking for another place to go fish. They wasn't even going to the truck, but I didn't know that at the time.

But sitting back there in that boat, I kinda looked at the bottom of that boat and there always was just a smidgen of water in the boat there and I didn't think nothing of it. We're going across that lake—it's a long ways across that lake—and I'm kinda still looking around at the beautiful morning. I look down there in the bottom of that boat, and I think dad-blamed it, it seemed like there's a little more water in this boat. I don't say nothing about it, and they ain't even looking back there at me—they're still looking where they're going. We drive along a little bit more across that lake, and I kinda put my eyes on the bottom of that boat, and now I know that dad-blamed-it—there's a right more water in the bottom of that boat than there was before. And I'm thinking, surely

Cowboy fishin'

to goodness, there ain't no leak in this boat—it was a good boat.

We drive along a little more when this gas can comes floating by me—and I'm just fixing to say something to them boys up there. They just happened to turn around and said, "Oh, my gosh—we've got a leak! Head for the shore!" And I mean, they flopped that boat around and they took off to where the shore was. They gave me a little one-gallon water jug and they told me to go to dipping, and dip as fast as I can. We were gonna drown out here in the middle of this dad-blamed lake, sure as the world. I got excited about that, and you talk about dipping—I commences to go to dipping. We make it all the way over there to the pickup. And when we loaded that boat—we didn't sink—but I was giving plumb out because I had been dipping out all that water. We get out of that stupid boat, and we load that boat on that trailer. And I don't know what we hit, but there was a split about three foot long in the bottom of that fiberglass boat. It's a wonder we hadn't sunk right out there in the middle of that lake—drowned for sure. It was the first—and the LAST time—that I ever went fishing out on that lake.

41

COWBOY BABYSITTER

This next story is for anyone with a child, or someone watching a child. Kids are so special. But when they can crawl, you can't take your eyes off them! And when they can walk, they can get away in a hurry. When we went to Abilene, my son was a year old, and Dee's job had her working many hours. He went to a daycare, but he also went with me a lot. When we would go to team ropings, I would park my truck by the arena fence in a way that a loose horse could not get in there. I made a shade and put toys there, and then I tied him to the fence. I stayed with him until they call my name to rope. I just didn't trust anyone to watch him, and he was perfectly safe from anything. I would rope a steer and come right back to him.

One truck down from me, two ladies drove in to watch the roping, and they thought it was just plumb awful to see him tied to the fence. They said this to me in a

Cowboy babysitter

not-so-nice way, and it made me mad. I said, "Have you two ever had kids or watched kids?" And they said, "Oh, no!" I proceeded to tell them to get out of here and leave us alone! And that they did.

My son had messed in his pants, and I had just started to fix that problem, when they called my name out to rope. And in rodeos or ropings, if they call you three times and you are not there, they will turn you out. My partner was on his horse, and I told him to run down there and see if they will drop us down a few ropers. He just yelled out, "He's changing a diaper!" and everyone laughed. The announcer, who knew me good, said, "That's okay, Mr. Mom, take your time. We'll just wait for you." So that's what I did. I got teased about it for a long time. But it didn't bother me at all. I love that boy!

42

THE DOCTOR

OUT THERE IN WEST TEXAS, in the little town of Snyder, me, my team-roping pardner—my good buddy—and my little boy, we go to a roping out in Lubbock. We roped up there all day long and they had a real, real good place there in Snyder—a restaurant called Shack. It's a great restaurant, and we'd ate there several times. We leave the roping, we're coming back through Snyder, and we sure are hungry. We pull up there at that restaurant, go in there, and have a great big, nice, good supper and then drive on home. We get home and the next morning —Monday morning—my wife is listening to the national news on TV. It says "If anybody has eaten at the Shack in Snyder, Texas, in the last two weeks—they've had an outbreak of hepatitis—and you need to get a hepatitis shot." Evidently, hepatitis is pretty serious—I don't know nothing about it—but it's pretty serious and you had

The doctor

better go get you a shot. That's what she tells me, and I said, "Okay, I guess I'll go."

Me, Ty, and my buddy that was with us, we all gotta go get a shot. He makes an appointment with his doctor, and he goes and gets his shot. I tell ol' Dee, I said, "Call Ty's pediatrician and make us an appointment for the next day. Make it first thing that morning and see if they can just go ahead and give me a shot so I don't have to go to some other old doctor. Just give me a shot right there." She does everything just fine, and they said, "Yeah, no problem. Both of you just come in first thing. You'll be very the first ones we see that morning." Me and that boy, we load up, and we go up there to that little doctor's office—there ain't nobody in the waiting room just yet. That nurse, she called us back there—said, "Come on back there in the office, and I'll give you both a shot."

My little boy—he's dreading it—he's about five, six years old, and he tells me, he said, "Oh Daddy, please let me go first and get it over with. I ain't had no sleep last night thinking about that shot. I know it's gonna hurt, but just please let me be first. I got to get it over with!" I told him okay, no problem. That nurse, she says, "It's got to go back in your hip. Just pull your britches down a little bit, and lay across your old daddy's lap." He did, and she popped that needle in his little rear end, giving him that shot. Man, he never cried, whimpered, or nothing. He stood up, pulled them britches up and said, "Okay Daddy —it's your turn now."

I stood up, pulled my britches down a little bit, and I

leaned over a counter. Now—I don't know why I did this, this was just mean, it was just mean, and I shouldn't have done it—I don't even know why I thought of it. But that little old nurse, when she stuck that needle in my butt, I squalled like a wild Comanche, just as loud as I could, and it scared that nurse. She jumped back, and my little boy yelled, "Daddy, she left that needle hanging out your butt!" She got mad—she cussed me. She said, "The waiting room, they all heard you holler! That waiting room is full of kids in there now. And we ain't never gonna get them kids back here in this office!"

She just jabbed that medicine in me—wasn't very nice about it—and she didn't need to be either. She just jabbed that medicine in me, in my butt, turned around, and stormed out of there yelling, "Get out of this doctor's office!" I pulled my britches up, and I walked through that waiting room—there's three or four little kids in there—and I was holding my hip and kinda limping out of there. And them kids were crying! I shouldn't have done that.

My wife got a call in about an hour at her office, and it was that doctor. He told her, said, "Whatever you do, do not EVER let that husband of yours come to this doctor's office again! We never got them kids back in there to treat them, they was crying so bad!" That was a mean thing to do and I deserved every bit of that, I guarantee you.

43

ACTING

THAT LITTLE BOY OF MINE, Ty, he wanted to act—do this acting deal. He did acting classes there in Abilene. Fooled around there and did some modeling, some real runway modeling. Did some little commercials, local commercials there, and he was kinda trying to pursue acting. He's five or six years old at the time.

The little acting coach teacher, once a year, she'd take some kids plumb-way up there to New York City. They had a competition up there: they had runway modeling to do, some kind of little acting deal, and show some kind of talent. And they're going to stay at the Waldorf Astoria Hotel in New York City. I didn't have no business up there in that city, so my wife went with him. They're going to be up for about four days, and I stayed home.

But we couldn't figure out what my little boy was going to do for talent. Some of them danced or sang—did this, that, and the other. I couldn't figure out what he was gonna do. Didn't think that boy had no talent for nothing. I wrote him a little speech that was going to be about a little boy, a little ranch cowboy growing up in West Texas —ya know—ranching and cowboying, with rattlesnakes, red ants, and all that. I write this little poem—and I ain't no poem writer—but somehow or another, it turned out real good. My wife found this old boy who wrote jingles for different commercials there in Abilene. He had him a little studio, so she contacts him and tells him we want him to write some music.

When Ty goes up there, they play this music tape. He comes out on the stage and the music kinda dies down. My little boy, he's going to say this speech—the music is playing real low in the background. They're up there in that Waldorf Astoria—the ballroom is full of people— several hundred people are there. He's got his black hat on. He screws that black hat on, his ears flop down there like he's gonna ride a bucking horse, and he comes out there with them britches stabbed in his boots, got his little rope, and he does a little trick roping. He walks out there on that big old stage and the music's going on in the background, and he gives that little old speech, and lo and behold, he wins the talent deal.

It surprised me, but that's what happened. He fooled around up there, and when they come back home, I was asking him all about it. Every morning when he'd go with me, we'd stop, and I'd have coffee somewhere. He'd have chocolate milk and a honey bun—that's what he liked for

Acting

breakfast. They got back home, and he told me all about this Waldorf Astoria Hotel and the whole trip and what kind of good time they had. I said, "Ty, do you think you wanna go around there—maybe move up there? Do we need to do that?" And he said, "Oh, no, Daddy! They ain't even got no place to build an arena up there. They got this place—some kind of ol big park—there in the middle of New York City. But we can't build one there. Besides that, they kill people there every night so we can't hang around there. Plus, the fact is, I looked around all over New York City for four days and there ain't no chocolate milk or a honey bun nowhere. So we don't wanna go up there!"

He come back and he pursued his acting career. Two colleges there in Abilene, their drama department, they used him several times to do little plays. They had them a little dinner play there, that was gonna last about a week. They go up there and they rehearse, and they're getting ready to do the opening night. We're sitting in the audience, and he's backstage, and I just happen to look up and I see his little head. There ain't hardly nobody in there yet, we're there early and two or three people are in that whole big audience. I see his little head sticking out behind that curtain, and he motioned for me to come back there. I wondered what he wanted, so I go back there. He said, "Daddy, we've been rehearsing this play for two weeks. And now, look, there ain't nobody out there in the audience. That's terrible!"

I said, "Well, that's right, Ty, but those people that are

out there in that audience—I don't know how many are going to show up. We're a little early—but they took their hard-earned money that they worked for all during the week, and they bought a ticket. It don't make no difference if there's one person out there or a thousand. They paid their money to come in here and see you perform. You do the best job you could do." So that's what he did, and of course, the whole place filled up by the time it started. That kind of took care of all that.

Later on, we carried him to a bunch of auditions. Got him an agent and carried him to a bunch of auditions here, there, and yonder—Dallas, San Antonio, Austin—he went to a lot of them. He had trouble getting a part. Finally—*finally*—he got a part. He's about fourteen years old and got him a part in a big Disney movie, *The Mighty Ducks*. I go to Hollywood with him. Dee stayed home, tended to everything, the cattle, and all that. We go out there to Hollywood, and they got us all fixed up in apartments and stuff. And we get there next day, here they come by, in this bus. There's fourteen of them kids and their parents—they pick us up, all of us—and the bus carries them to wardrobe, gotta get their clothes all figured out. We unload over there, they all go into this place. I'm standing outside, trying to stay out of the way, drinking a cup of coffee, all that.

Ty, he ain't in there but probably about ten minutes, he comes outside in just a pair of wranglers, barefooted, and he ain't got no shirt on. He comes up to me, and he says, "Daddy, I can't do this." I said, "What do you mean you can't do this? You've been trying to do this whole thing—done all these auditions—all these years of schooling, and all that kind of stuff. Said you wanted to be an actor and stuff. What do you mean you can't do this?" He said, "You oughta see the stupid clothes they want me to wear."

He's supposed to be—and this don't make no sense anyway—he's supposed to be a Texas cowboy that's playing hockey. Now, I don't understand that part of it, but that's what the script said. About that time, three old gals, they come out there, and two of them I couldn't understand—they didn't speak too good of English. This other one, she's yelling at me, and I said, "What seems to be the problem?"

"Your son doesn't like the clothes that we've got him to wear." Ty says, "Yeah, you oughta see these stupid boots that look like some dingo boots and rings. Then, they got some stupid hat with a bunch of quail feathers on it!" They'd done their best to try and figure out what a little Texas cowboy wears. And I said, "Well, ma'am, what the boy got on when he come in here—that's what a Texas cowboy wears ... his black hat, his boots, belt buckle, and all that. That's what a Texas cowboy wears." She said, "Can you come in here and look at these catalogs to pick him out some clothes?" I said, "Yeah—that ain't no problem." So I do that, and everything's just fine and dandy.

Now it comes time to do the ice-skating thing. They

gotta learn to ice skate, and that's for the first two months. We're there, and that first week, all these ladies—there's thirteen ladies and me—thirteen mamas and me! Well, them ladies, they don't have much to do with me. A couple of them were busy pretty good, and the rest of them—they got their nose kinda stuck in the air. Anyhow, we're all sitting around—of course, all you do is just sit there all day long—and visit.

At the time there's a commercial on TV that I watched every morning, and I never had heard of this before—but the commercial, it was something like a laxative that people take called Perdiem. That's the name of the laxative. I never had heard of that before—I had just seen it on the commercial might near every morning that week. Just sitting around there all day, that Friday, I hear two of these women ask if they'd seen that guy coming around that's supposed to bring our per diem. This one this lady says no, but that he's supposed to come today. I don't know what the deal is, but one says, "I hope he shows up today because I'm sure needing it." And another says, "Me too, I sure need it." I didn't know why or what they was talking about. Then another one says, "Yeah. I think you're supposed to be here, and after a while, he's bringing everybody their per diem."

And I'm thinking why in the world is this guy bringing this laxative here to all these women, and all of us, and no one said nothing about it. Finally, of course, dumb me, I speak up. I said, "What in the world's the

Acting

matter with all you women?" Asked why you gotta have this laxative, Perdiem. They said, "Laxative? Per diem is our money that they're supposed to bring, and we're supposed to live on every week, all week long!" I didn't have no idea what "per diem" was, 'cuz I hadn't heard of nothing like that before. But he comes, they get a big laugh out of that, and the guy comes with the money and gives everybody their per diem, and I take mine too.

They're ice skating—they learn how to ice skate real good—and they start the movie. They start that old movie up, and they're filming every day. One particular time, about a month later, they got to do some filming down there on Venice Beach. I never had been on Venice Beach before, and we all get down there. They're going to film there all week long. All you can do on a movie set is just try to stay out of the way. Now, there's this one gal, and she's kinda the ramrod of all them kids, and us. Tells us where to go, just exactly where to be, and to stay out of the way. She's helping—she's real nice and sweet and all that. There's a lot of things going on at Venice Beach—with these weird people that I ain't never seen before—and I'm seeing the sights.

That goes on for, I don't know, long about four days or so. We're at this one particular place on Venice Beach, and I finally get kind of used to seeing all the people and the sights and all that. And there's a sidewalk—about a six-foot-wide sidewalk—that these people, they're on rollerblades. They're dressed in suits, and they're coming to work—that's the way they come to work—on them rollerblades, right down that sidewalk. I thought that's kinda strange to come down through there every morning, and go back every evening when they get off work.

The prop truck over there was a big eighteen-wheeler that had all the movie props in there that they need. And this ol boy—he was head of that prop truck—I'd walk by and visit with him like I visited with everybody on set. I'd noticed a bicycle in that prop truck. I went over and I asked that ol gal, I said, "What's the deal with this walkway? Everybody's coming down here on this concrete walkway." And she said, "Yeah—that's called a boardwalk. It runs about twenty miles up and down this beach." I asked her, I said, "Well, I'm kinda tired of hanging around here. Reckon I can get that bicycle and ride up that deal a little ways up the beach—to see what things look like up there?" She said, "Yeah, if you don't go too awfully far—don't go but a couple of miles or something—turn around and come back. You need to kind of be hanging around on this set."

I said that was okay—that ain't no big deal. I'm dressed just like I always do—hat, boots—dressed cowboy. And of course, everybody looked at me as funny as I looked at them idiots there on Venice Beach. But I get on that bicycle—I can ride a bicycle real good—so I take off on that bicycle. Unbeknownst to me, my son, when I take off on that bicycle, he tells the producer and director, he said, "Y'all might want to film this—him—my daddy

Acting

riding that bicycle. It might be more interesting than doing this movie!"

The whole movie set—I didn't know it—but they're watching me ride off on this bicycle with my hat on, my boots on, and all that. I don't get but fifty feet down there—and there's always people riding their bicycles up and down that thing all the time. Here come an ol gal in one of them bee-kinis, a butt-floss bee-kini, and she's riding a bicycle. She's going somewhere on it, and she's meeting me—we're gonna have to pass each other head on.

And she's got a bicycle like an old droop-horn cow—she's got them "handlebars" drooped down there. And she's leaned over it –it looks very uncomfortable to me—but she's leaned over a-pedaling that bicycle. She meets up there with me and we pass, and she's got that little bee-kini on. She had them "things there in the front" flopping around, and when she went by me, I kinda looked over my shoulder and her rear end is sticking up in the air. And I'm looking at that and when I do—I didn't realize it at the time—but when I looked around, my shoulders turned the front wheel of that bicycle. I'm a-pedaling pretty good—and the tire hit that beach sand. And I mean, it flipped me. That bicycle bucked me off—and it bent—I bent the front wheel of that bicycle. I look back there and that whole dad-blamed movie set is a-laughing—my son, he's a-laughing—the whole bunch is laughing.

I get up and dust myself off, and the front wheel of that bicycle is bent. So I put my feet on it and I put my hand on it, and I pull that front wheel back up straight. I get back on it and I'm riding it back to that prop truck, but it ain't going too good. It's kinda wobbling in the front end. But I flew around there, and I give that bicycle back to that prop-truck guy. I said, "Whatever you do, don't you let me ride that bicycle ever again!" That was all for my bicycle riding, but at least they all had a big laugh out of that.

44

RODEO RAPPIN'

I'D ENDED my musical career long time ago—when I was two years old—as I told ya earlier. But one night, we were coming back from a rodeo. It was about the time that everybody—all these rappers—they started rapping this kind of music. Rapping here and rapping there, rapping everywhere, but there wasn't nobody that did nothing about rodeo or western things. We were driving, near the end of the day, and we laughed about all that and we thought somebody oughta have a rodeo rap. Rapping about rodeo and western stuff. Didn't one of us think to say no more about it. About two or three months went by, and the subject kind of come up again amongst us anyhow.

One night, I woke up about two o'clock in the morning. Couldn't sleep, couldn't figure out why I couldn't sleep. I just couldn't. So I went and made a pot of coffee. I'm thinking about what I'm going to do that day and all that stuff. Then something hit my brain about this rapping. Now, I've never done anything like this before—in my entire life—I ain't no songwriter, I ain't no singer, but I got me a pad and a pencil. I'm drinking that coffee, sitting at the kitchen table, and I go to writing this song. It's called "Rodeo Rapping"—I come up with that name. It goes through every event of rodeo, in a rap form. I'm writing this thing and I'm just writing one word right after other—one event right after another—and I'm surprising myself. I can't even figure out what I'm doing.

I admire songwriters because they got the talent to do that stuff. It's just amazing to me—I ain't got no talent for it! But I write this thing and I'm just doing all the goods. Everything's getting to be daylight, and we've gotta take Ty to a little old rodeo somewhere. I get stumped at the bull riding part—can't think of it no more—so I quit writing. Ty's back there getting ready, Dee, she said, "Was you sick last night?" I said no, and she said, "I heard you get up and you didn't come back. What'd you do?" I said, "Oh, I was just writing a song." And she said, "WHAT?! What do you mean, writing a song?" I said, "Yes, I'm writing a song." She said, "What? I've heard everything now!"

I go out there, load the horses up because we're getting ready—we gotta go to a rodeo. We load them horses, get in the truck, and here we go. We take off. I get about halfway down to that rodeo, about an hour and a half, maybe two hours down the road. And I pull off the interstate. I pull over. And Dee said, "What's the matter? We got a flat?"

And I said, "No—I thought of the rest of that song. You're going to have to drive while I write it."

She said that's the craziest thing she'd ever heard of—anyhow, I made her drive. I picked it right back up and finished writing that dad-blamed song about the bull riding. By the time we get to the rodeo, we ain't got time to even talk about it no more—we do the rodeo thing, and after, she said, "I gotta hear this song that you've written." I said, "Well, now you can't hear it just yet." I get her to call that old boy who had done that writing for the little old jingle for Ty when he went to New York City. She called him up to see if he's still in that studio—and he was—so I told him I've got this song and I need you to put music to it. He said, "Get up here!"

I go up there and spend all night there in that studio while he done all the music. First thing I told him when I went in there, I said, "Look, I've been married a long time, and I've team roped up my whole life. When I do this little song—the words of this song—if you think that's the stupidest thing you ever heard of, then just tell me and I'll throw that in the trash and I'll get out of your hair." He sets a little microphone in front of me and says, "Do it." I get into that song—a little tune—kinda a rap-form deal, and I'm talking fast. He stops me in a little bit. He said, "That's the dang-dest thing I ever heard. That's awesome. We gotta get some music to that." I walk out of there a little bit before daylight with a tape.

He'd done all the music to it. We put it all together in that studio that night. I get back home—Dee's in bed—

and I crawl back in bed. It ain't quite daylight yet, but I'm tired and give out, and she says, "You do it?" And I said yes. She says, "Get the tape—I gotta hear that tape!" So, we're sitting out there in the garage, in the pickup, and we plug that tape in. She's listening to "Rodeo Rapping"—and she liked it. It was a funny little old song.

I have it around there and I play it, but I won't tell people who in the world done it. I play it for different people—my customers listen to it—and they say man, "That's neat!" or "That's good." I don't tell them who's done it, but I didn't know what to do with it. Finally, one thing led to another, and I sent it off to a radio station and this and that—another off here and there and yonder—and I can't get nothing done with it. It's really not a song to go on the radio, 'cuz it's got lots of terms about rodeo. If you don't understand rodeo, you don't understand a lot of the words in it. I didn't know what to do with it, so I sent it to rodeo announcers all over the country. And they had played that thing when people's coming into or setting down, or when they get up to get ready to leave—well, they're playing it.

The rodeo kids, they loved it! I sold several of them things over the next three or four years. It turned out really pretty good. I can't do the whole song here, but it kinda went something like this—started out with: *We come together this beautiful day, to watch the oldest sport in the USA. So come on, folks, get your feet a-tapping because you're gonna hear a little rodeo rapping.*

That's the way it started, and it went through every

event—it done real good. Like I say, that's the only song I've wrote—I tried to write another two, but I don't have the talent for it. That's about all of my songwriting, but we had a lot of fun with it. Been thinking about bringing it back and trying to sell it again after several years. I might. I might not.

45

GUTS AND OVERCOMING

At these charity fundraiser rodeos that we was going to, there was a guy that comes to them, and his story is absolutely amazing. It's very, very hard to believe, but it's true—all these stories I've told you are true—but this guy, he lived in East Texas, and he was a schoolteacher. He and his wife both were—and he roped—roped pretty good. But later on in years, he had diabetes and the diabetes got his sight, the boy went blind cause of his diabetes. Now, that's got to be very devastating to any individual, but he sat around since he was blind and moped around the house for two or three years. He and his wife's life—they were just in awful states—he felt sorry for himself.

Thank goodness for his wife. She came in from teaching school one day and he was moping around the house. She said, "You know, I'm sick of you. It's very unfortunate what's happened, but we gotta live our lives, and we gotta go on, and we gotta hold our head up, and we gotta get over this.' She said, 'I want you to go to the barn—I want you to go to rope a dummy—do something! But get off this couch and do something!"

He said, "I can't rope the dummy. I'm blind." And she said, "I don't care how you do it—go out there and try." Now, he could get to the barn—he knew how to get to the barn. He got that white cane, and to make a long story short, this guy, he roped that dummy, and roped that dummy, and roped that dummy, and got to where he could rope off a horse.

I don't understand all this, really, but when he'd go to a roping, they would tie a little bell between that steer's horns and somehow or another—it had to be a God thing—that horse and him could focus in on that bell and he could rope them horns on all them steers. It was absolutely amazing. He could rope pretty dad-gum-good. That actor putting on them celebrity rodeos, he heard about him, and they got him to come to them celebrity rodeos. That's where I really met the guy, and like I say, his story is absolutely phenomenal!

They had one of these charity rodeos in Abilene, Texas, where I lived—my hometown. Two or three different times over the years, I'd bring horses—team roping horses and them things—for them actors and singers to ride and rope on. I brought some horses up there and Ty, he's in the deal, that celebrity roping. A real famous rodeo announcer—he'd done real well, he's world famous—he's announcing this celebrity rodeo. And sometimes in them little old team ropings—it's just a draw pot, you put your name in there—and they draw the headers and the heelers. Then match them up together. Well, two or three different times over the years, they didn't draw up just right in some place. And they'd asked me to either head a steer, heel a steer, or something, to make the teams come out even.

My son comes over to me and said, "Hey, Daddy, you're going to have to head or heel—somebody didn't come out even." I said okay, it's just a draw pot. My son comes over there and said, "You drawed up with this old boy that's blind." I said, "Okay, fine then." I knew all about him—seen him rope before. Well, I get on my horse, and I go over there and I told him, I said, "You drawed up with me, and I don't know whether that's good or bad for you anyway. What do you need me to do to help you?" He said, "You just sit over here by me on your horse. And when they call our names out, you help me ride—show me kinda how to ride in the box—to turn around. When I rope that steer, you holler at me to turn off. When you heel him and it's time for me to face, you holler at me again, and I'll face." I said okay—no big deal.

It comes time for us to rope. They ain't got but about fifteen to twenty teams, something like that. You gotta rope two steers. The rodeo announcer announces this guy's name and tells his story, about how this man that's fixing to rope—head this steer—is blind. And talks about how he has worked hard, and he's got back to roping, and nobody can really understand how he can do this, but he ropes well now. He don't say nothing about me—which he ain't supposed to anyway—I ain't no celebrity anyhow, about nothing.

The crowd—the Abilene coliseum is full of people. That guy, he nods his head, and they open that gate, we run out there, and he ropes that steer, and I holler at him. He turns off, and I heel the steer, and I holler at him to face and man, the crowd goes absolutely berserk. They're screaming and hollering—standing up—a standing ovation and all that. It's just remarkable. They're going crazy in there about this. We go to the stripping chute to get his rope off. We come back—I think there are about five teams that caught—and we're one of them. We get to rope our second steer. Now, I have roped my whole life, and I ain't never really gotten nervous about roping. But basically, all we gotta do is ride in that chute, and if we catch this second steer, we're going to win that little team roping. It don't dawn on me until I ride in the box—we ride in the box—and when I turned my horse around, it hit me like a ton of bricks. Like all of a sudden, I got nervous because here I am, in my hometown, and all we got to do is catch this steer. And if this blind guy ropes him, and if I miss the heels, I'll never be able to live it down. I'll have to move plumb outta the United States, because I'll catch flak from that for the rest of my life.

That guy nods his head, and he comes out and he ropes at that steer. He catches one horn, and I holler at him ... I said, "Fish. Fish. Fish!" And he fished it on his nose, so I said, "You got him." And as he turned off, when he pulled his slack, it come off of the steer's nose and he got away. We ride out the back of the arena—it's out there in the dark—and this old boy tell me, he said, "Oh, Bob, I'm sorry I missed that steer. I just wanted to win that roping so bad. They were giving some beautiful buckles away." And of course—my smart mouth—I said, "How'd you know they were beautiful? You can't see them." He said, "My wife told me they was beautiful. And I wanted to win them so bad."

This guy was—he is one great, great, great individual. He jokes about his blindness and he's just a lot of fun and all that. Tease each other and get teased and tease everybody else. We're still riding along, and he said, "Oh, I wanted to win it so bad. I'm sorry that I missed that steer." And I said, "Of course. You oughta be! I ain't never roping with you ever again." He said, "Well, I told you I was sorry."

I said, "Stop your horse. You don't understand. Do you realize that if you had caught that steer, and turned him, and I had a-missed, do you realize that I woulda had to leave the United States?" He said, "Oh, yeah, I didn't think about that. I made you look real good, didn't I?" I told him that he sure enough did!

That guy lives in New Mexico now—he was one awesome individual! And I think about every time I do miss a steer—I think about that, here he is, blind, and can catch them things, and I got two good eyes, and I still miss and mess up.

PARTING WORDS

That's a mess of stories—about all I can think of now. Hopefully you might've learned about what not to do, and think real good before you do anything. I'm seventy-something years old—maybe if I live another seventy-something years, I'll come up with that many stories and write another book.

I hope you enjoyed the lil read. That's all I want you folks reading these stories in this little old book to do. All I can say to you is that living your life is all about friendship, fun, family, love, and laughter. Live every day just like it's your last.

Thanks. I shore would like to meet you someday and shake your hand. Stay safe, have fun, be kind to all. Have a great day, every day, and enjoy the rest of your life.

They call me Cowboy Bob McClary.

THANK YOUS

First of all, I realize that I am a very fortunate and blessed individual, my whole life. Beginning with two of the best parents anyone could ever have. They both were very supportive and encouraging about anything I ever did, but the most important thing is they loved me with all their hearts and showed it all the time. And all of those same traits carried on when I got married to my wife, Dee, a woman who is like them in every way. When you have a spouse that loves and likes you, you can handle anything that life, people, or the world throws at you. I also happen to have the best son, Ty, and daughter-in-law, Christie, as well as the most wonderful granddaughter, Marley Mae, in the world. That makes me a very RICH MAN!

To Dr. Frank Lawlis—thank you for inspiring this idea and prodding me to sit down and put into words the stories of my life thus far.

Thank Yous

To Teri Gentry—thank you for taking my voice and putting it on paper for all to read.

www.ingramcontent.com/pod-product-compliance
Lightning Source LLC
Chambersburg PA
CBHW030447100526
44580CB00002B/25